A BOOK & A LOVE AFFAIR

Other books by Helen Bevington

Doctor Johnson's Waterfall

(1946)

Nineteen Million Elephants

(1950)

A Change of Sky

(1956)

When Found, Make a Verse Of

(1961)

Charley Smith's Girl

(1965)

A
BOOK
&

HELEN BEVINGTON

Harcourt, Brace & World, Inc.

New York

To B.

A LOVELY COUPLE

By more rotundity than now,
A few sparse hairs above your brow,
By my abundance manifest
In amplitude not yet possessed,
We shall be mocked. We shall have been,
You will recall, once young, once thin,
Once lissome, gloriously supple.
We shall have been a lovely couple.

So woo me now, before that time,
While yet we glitter in our prime,
While the discovered world is green
And we are verdant too and lean.
Say, say you love me. Oh, make haste
While we have vocables to waste,
While we have syllables to spare.
Speak volumes of this love affair.

A BOOK & A LOVE AFFAIR

1

I sat down in the seat beside him one morning in Professor Hunter Wright's class in Romanticism. And that was how my life began. The same evening, on our first date, B. and I spent it riding back and forth all night on the ferry. It was the old Fort Lee ferry at 125th Street in Manhattan, which took us churning over to Edgewater, New Jersey, from pier to pier in about eight minutes, then after a while tooted its whistle, clanked the ferry chain, and brought us back again. A round trip including loading and reloading of vehicles lasted thirty minutes, though I think the service slowed up to one an hour after midnight.

We might have stopped off to ride the roller coaster at Palisades Amusement Park. Instead, B. kept paying our five-cent fares, back and forth, back and forth across the Hudson River as many times as it took, all the lovely night long till the early-morning rush hour. We sat inside the ferry cabin on a hard wooden bench where we couldn't whiff the sea air or watch the shore lights. I don't remember a moon. It was too bitter cold anyway on February 7 to stand under the moon on the deck of a double-ender. The winter wind had stung our faces and blown my hair wildly that evening when we came aboard. It was too raw and windy out there for falling in love.

We looked at each other and talked all night, breath to breath, hands touching. During the owl hours from, say, 2:00 to 6:00 A.M. we had the boat more or less to ourselves. One thing that naturally occurred to us was Edna St. Vincent Millay's love poem about riding back and forth all night on the ferry. In 1927 we were graduate students in English at Columbia University—why wouldn't we know her poem? It probably gave us the idea in the first place of a way to spend the night together, though Walt Whitman was a rider of the New York ferries too. On Miss Millay's excursion, she and her love were very tired and very merry, to rhyme with ferry. She said the one they crossed on smelled like a stable and the wind was cold.

"Maybe it was the same ferry," I said to B.

He turned briefly from gazing into my eyes to inspect the bare, dark-brown, starkly lit interior. An old man lay stretched out asleep in the corner, his face streaked with dirt, his tin lunchbox on the seat beside him. A list of fares was posted on the wall—for an extra nickel you could wheel a baby carriage or lead a sheep or hog over to New Jersey. There was a smear of spit on the dirty floor and some torn pieces of newspaper. The place smelled stale, more like a urinal than a stable, more of people than of horses.

"She took the Staten Island ferry," B. said. "Anyway, it's a terrible poem." He was six years older than I, that I had already found out, and I was twenty. He had taught school

4

before coming last fall to earn a doctor's degree at Columbia. Things were clear to him. He was used to saying whether a poem was good or bad.

Yet here I sat passionately devoted to the works of Edna St. Vincent Millay, a loyal follower of hers. I owned her books, envied her love affairs, and knew this ferry poem by heart. "What's wrong with it?" I asked in surprise.

"It doesn't ring true. It's too damned *poetic*. She says they went back and forth all night on the ferry, but at the same time she has them lying on a hilltop till the dawn came. 'And the sun rose dripping, a bucketful of gold.' Jesus. To rhyme with cold."

B. was absolutely right about the sun. It didn't rise like a bucketful of gold for us. The dawn came up dripping mist and fog, a dismal gray winter dawn. When we finally stepped off the ferry at 125th Street on our last lurching, creaking trip round, a dozen foot passengers pushed and shoved past us, hurrying to work. They looked like the ones who had crossed with us last night to sleep in their beds in New Jersey.

On solid ground again, B. and I stumbled with weariness. We yawned violently and laughed, turning to walk arm in arm the few blocks up Broadway back to our rooms. He lived in a men's dormitory on campus, John Jay Hall. I had a single room on 120th Street with a Columbia professor of Spanish and his family, the Callcotts. After the exemplary life I had lived since moving in with them last October, how would I explain this immorality of staying out all night with a man? Perhaps I could slip into the apartment before they woke and found me missing.

As we walked, the fog hid and enveloped us. We were alone, crossing under the girders of the I.R.T. Broadway-Seventh Avenue line with a train roaring overhead. Suddenly B. stopped and took me in his arms, or did I pause a second before he did? He held me close, kissing me hard on the mouth. Again and again he kissed me, and with eyes shut I held on and kissed him back.

"I love you," he said at last. "Why have I taken all night to tell you so?"

"I don't know," I said. "I love you. It's been a long night waiting to be told."

At the entrance to my apartment house, we stood at the foot of the steps clinging desperately to each other, as if a train were moving away with the conductor shouting "All aboard," as if we might never meet again. B.'s face was pale with love and lack of sleep. He was trembling with love.

"I have to go now, darling. Forgive me. I've got to run over to my room and pack my bag," he said, and his voice shook.

"Oh, my God," I cried in despair, "are you leaving town?"

"I'm going to marry you," he said, kissing my mouth. "Let's see. I can be back in half an hour. Will you be ready by then?"

I looked at my wristwatch. Seven o'clock. I looked marveling at him. "I'll see you in class this morning," I said. "Bring your notebook, not your suitcase. We can't get married today."

"Why not, in God's name?"

"I'll tell you later."

I left him and ran up the steps into the apartment building. The colored elevator man, just coming on duty, stopped me in the hall.

"No kissing on the front piazza, if you please, miss," he said, with a broad grin. "You know what the tenants'll do. They'll look out their windows and some old gal she's bound to see you at it and, boy, will she give me hell!"

6

I laughed and rushed up the stairs, up two flights, letting myself stealthily into the Callcotts' apartment.

*

B. went to his room in John Jay Hall and packed his traveling bag, putting into it a new pair of blue-striped pajamas. So he told me a little later as we sat side by side in Emery Neff's graduate course in Victorian Literature. By some miracle we were taking the same courses, reading the same books, listening to the same fabulous words together.

Since last October I had seen his face every day in my classrooms in Philosophy Hall and Havemeyer. I had watched for him to enter and find a seat, usually beside some attractive girl with whom he would talk and laugh before the lecture. He laughed a great deal, this slender, boyish, lighthaired young man of medium height, with heavy dark eyebrows and warm gray eyes. I knew his face by heart, dreamed of it—the straight nose, the quizzical look, the immense charm, the sensuous yet neatly curved mouth into which as class ended he quickly thrust a cigarette. His smile really dazzled.

I had sat opposite him in Carpenter Library, at a table where he read too absorbed to glance in my direction, or wandered over to joke with the pretty woman at the desk, a flirt and an emptyhead. A beautiful graduate student named Linda studied in the library at whom he used to stare fixedly. And there was Queen Marie of Romania, who visited the Columbia campus in October. When she took the arm of President Nicholas Murray Butler and swept grandly down the red carpet spread to welcome her, well, B. was in the crowd staring at her too. He was a noticing man.

Then after four long months, on a Monday, February 7, 1927, my luck finally changed. On that day when the Em-

7

peror of Japan was buried, King George V opened Parliament, and Coolidge was President, I walked down the aisle of Professor Hunter Wright's class in Romanticism. The only empty seat in the room was next to B.

"Won't you sit down, Miss Smith?" he said politely, but he didn't need to. I had made a dive for it and was there, seated before the words (how did he know my name?) escaped his mouth. So far as I was concerned, I had arrived for good through the intervention of the gods—an immovable object, not to leave his side again.

*

The next day, after the allnight ferry ride and the falling in love, we had no sleep. We sat bemused through two classes and ate a sandwich on a cold park bench in Morningside Park, then read in the library or tried to, holding hands in a tight grip under the table.

After supper in a cafeteria, where we drank black coffee to keep awake, B. came with me to the Callcotts' apartment. I hadn't brought a man to my room before. To help pay my rent I looked after three-year-old Mary Callcott three evenings a week while her parents were out. Mrs. Callcott attended evening classes in University Extension, and Professor Callcott worked in his office. When I had put Mary to bed, B. and I had the apartment to ourselves. We sat side by side on my daybed and began to talk at last on the subject of marriage.

By now I felt stupefied by fatigue, nearly unconscious, barely able to prop my eyes open. All I wanted was to lie down beside B. and close my eyes, obviously what he wanted himself. But we hadn't reached that stage of lovemaking. We had some talking still to do.

"You wouldn't marry me today," B. said. "Why not?"

"You didn't ask me. It is an honor that I dreamed not of."

"I told you I was going over to pack my bag. And by

8

God I meant it. And by God I intend to keep it packed till you marry me. Will you marry me tomorrow?"

"Oh, darling, darling—"

"This is a strictly formal offer. My love, look at me. I'm proposing to you now."

"I can't."

"Can't what?"

"Oh, for heaven's *sake,* B.! You know what we're talking about—marriage. I can't marry you, not tomorrow, not the day after, not ever. I can't *ever* marry you. I can't *marry!*"

"Are you already married?"

"No, of course not."

"That's it, then," B. said. "You've got to marry somebody unless you want to turn into a wispy dried-up graduate student." He relaxed and lay back with eyes closed, half dozing against the wall. "You know, it's a queer thing. Till last night I had made up my mind not to marry, either. I planned to give myself body and soul to women graduate students—the ones who never had a date in their lives, the godforsaken homely ones, you know the type, who have lost hope. I was going to make love to them. They'd have a man at least once before too late."

"How many have you made happy so far?" I asked.

"You're the first on my list, Miss Smith. The service starts with you."

"Oh, B., stop it," I said. "You and your benevolence to virgins. Listen to me before I fall asleep. *Listen.* I can't marry you because I don't *believe* in marriage. I believe in love, naturally, that's different, but I don't *believe* in changing my name or giving up my freedom. What's more, I don't want to have children—not any at all. Not in a frightful world like this. I've made up my mind. I'm not going to marry anybody!"

I studied B.'s face closely to see if he accepted the finality of my terms. He looked unimpressed to the point of seeming drugged. His eyes were glazed, he started to drowse off. Rousing himself with a jerk, he yawned furiously in my face and shook and pounded his head to keep awake.

"Poor darling," he muttered, slumping forward against me and closing his eyes. This time he was going, gone. Then his voice returned faintly, began to trail away. "I love you. . . . I want you . . . and . . . I want a wife and ten children."

He fell back with a thud on the bed, pulled me down beside him on the pillow, put his arms around me, and we both immediately fell sound asleep. At nine o'clock when Mrs. Callcott returned from her class, she let herself in with a key, walked down the hall past my open door, and discovered the two of us lying on my bed wrapped in each other's arms. Her first horrified thought was no doubt of little Mary's morals.

"Miss Smith!" she cried sharply, and her outraged voice woke us up.

*

I found another room two blocks away on 118th Street in a building where the landlady, an elderly complaining widow with the shape of a pickle fork, lived on the ground floor and rented out her drab little rooms at six dollars a week to whoever applied, no credentials asked. Next to me on the fourth floor lived Mr. Webb, a professional bridge player, who seldom returned to his room before dawn. On the other side was the bathroom, posted with heavy admonitions in the landlady's bold and exasperated handwriting: "Turn off the light!" "Clean out the tub!" "Throw nothing in the toilet!" "Pick up your towel!" "*Please* be a little more considerate of others!" Down the narrow hall in their separate cubicles, the other roomers were Rita, a black-eyed Puerto Rican girl taking languages at Columbia; beyond her a middleaged traveling man; and at the end of the hall Doris and Pauline, two amiable nurses enrolled at Teachers College who worked part-time at St. Luke's Hospital. Both of them were going steady. Rita had a lover named Carlos.

B. and I were free now to spend our days and nights together, our lives in fact, with nobody to care. The landlady's rules strictly forbade the cooking or hoarding of food in one's room. She said nothing in her vexed public notices about entertaining a man there. B. went home after midnight, perhaps to spend the rest of the night playing auction bridge with his friends in John Jay Hall, the only way he managed to enjoy anyone's society but mine. He talked of taking me to his dormitory room to meet the boys, but since the visit required my dressing in men's clothes, being spirited up in the elevator to the sixth floor, and being expelled from the University if caught, I put off going.

We sat breathless through our classes, fevered with love, trying to attend our learned professors and at the same time carry on a passionate courtship. My lecture notes, taken during the first four months with meticulous care—in John Erskine's course in Materials of Poetry, in Carl Van Doren's Friday-afternoon literary gossip on the modern American scene—went completely to pieces. Even my handwriting changed for the worse as we wrote love messages up and down the margins of our notebooks.

"Give all to love, Obey thy heart," B. wrote, quoting from a poem of Emerson's, and I replied in kind from Swinburne: "Ask nothing more of me, sweet, All I can give you I give."

He wooed me with the beautiful eloquent lines from Piers Plowman:

I will swynk and sweat and sow for us both
And labor for love of you half of my lifetime.

And I would wonder how to answer him and come up with, oh, Marvell:

The grave's a fine and private place,
But none, I think, do there embrace.

Our heads were brimful of quotations, such is the power of poetry over existence. We spent the hours in class making love in the language of English poetry, American, French, German, whatever words and authors we knew. Our standards, I think, were reasonably high. Now and then I objected to a burning passage of his as being too sentimental, not to my taste.

"I quake," he wrote once, "with unutterable desire."

"Rubbish," I wrote firmly underneath. "Nobody has ever made you quake."

If I happened to quote from a poet he didn't fancy—Louis Untermeyer, for example:

Never will you let me
Tire of leaping passion,
Never can I grow weary
Of undesired joys,

B. was only too glad to give me his honest opinion.

"Merciful Christ in Heaven," he wrote in the margin of my notebook, "but your taste is low."

We spent a couple of class periods one afternoon playing a word game begun by accident when I quoted a line from Elinor Wylie's recent novel, *The Venetian Glass Nephew:* "And then he wept a little, and fell to talking of magic and macaroni." B. idly added two more words beginning with *m-a* that one might weep a little to talk about—madams and Machiavelli—and the game began, each taking a dizzy turn at it: maidens and marsupials, mating and maraschino cherries, magnolias and madrigals, Mama and the Mason-Dixon Line. I was pleased with myself for thinking of Mae West and Mary Magdalene. But B.'s wits were quick, he was always cleverer than I. Macbeth and maple syrup, he wrote, and on we went: Magna Charta and *magna cum laude,* marriage and marrowbones, Mrs. Malaprop and major league baseball, magnanimity and magistrates.

Till I ran out of vocabulary. For one thing, a pair of words got in my way that in self-respect I refused to write down. Finally they were the last two left in my head, I could dredge up no more. As in a game of chess, I sat over my next move hoping for divine help. B. should be ready to give up too, though he looked perfectly confident and unworried. What other lousy words started with *m-a?*

"Let's switch to *d-e,*" I wrote to get myself off the hook, offering a few tempting examples: deists and delirium, death and deliverance, devyllysshely devysed.

"*M-a* or nothing," B. answered, shaking his head sternly. "Don't weasel out now. Play the game!"

With a deep sigh I slowly wrote my final entry: masturbation and maidenheads. B. exploded with a laugh that rocked the classroom. In the midst of his sober lecture, probably on William Dean Howells, Professor Rusk looked up from his notes in pained astonishment. We sat convulsed, gasping in spasms of laughter.

But then every day B. wrote me a note in plain ordinary English. It was always the same—"My love, will you marry me?" And my reluctant answer was the same to him. I turned my head away. "No," I said. No.

When spring came with its April days, we cut class and walked beside the Hudson, taking along a book and a love affair.

"What shall we read?" B. would ask. "Foxe's *Book of Martyrs?*"

I didn't care for the panting words of *The Rubáiyát* ("Who is the Potter, pray, and who the Pot?"), but I was willing to listen any time to *Atalanta in Calydon* or *The*

Faerie Queene. On a bench in Riverside Park among the pigeons and seagulls, B. read aloud the whole of Browning's *The Ring and the Book*, which had the advantage of being interminable and so repetitious that I could gaze out at the passing barges on the silver river, or up at the Fort Lee ferryboats on their way to New Jersey, and think how terribly I loved him.

I remember our walking one day on Amsterdam Avenue and glancing up at an enormous sign that ran across the top of a brick building we were passing: "A Home for Aged, Indigent, and Respectable Females of the City of New York."

"That's where you'll end your miserable days unless you marry me," B. said.

"They won't let me in," I said.

"Why not?"

"See what it says? No whores allowed. You have to be respectable."

"Then marry, in the name of God," he said, like Pantagruel.

I bought a red dress to go dancing with him in the Harlem hot spots—Small's Paradise on Seventh Avenue or the Savoy Ballroom on Lenox, where you heard Chick Webb and the terrific beat of the hottest jazz in town, and the ballroom shook to the sweating performers of the black bottom. Nothing mattered but that he held me tight and whispered words of love in my ear; I was weak in the knees for love. Once or twice we went to the 125th Street burlesque where he showed me the strippers and teasers with their professional bumps and grinds. I found the whole thing hair-raising.

"They're so utterly damned moral!" I cried in amazement.

"Is that better than immoral?" B. asked.

"Certainly not, darling. Look at those poor undesirable girls."

14

We were looking at them as they galloped past in G strings, all but naked, down the long runway beside our seats. We saw their flabby breasts and bellies—those aging, pitiful, unlovely old girls with bulging thighs pierced by the thrust of a hypodermic needle. They had desperate fixed smiles on their faces, and they scared me. Poor, dreary, tired burlesque queens, they seemed the most sexless and tawdry lot of females in the world.

"Watch them two nights in a row and you'd be unsexed forever," I said. "They're a hellfire sermon on sin."

"Not to me they aren't," B. said.

*

That was the nature of the wooing. Otherwise we worked, with a formidable amount to do—especially B., who as a confirmed reader of English literature all his life had so far made the mistake of reading it for pleasure. The method had left gaps. After majoring in chemistry at Muskingum College in Ohio, he had taught mathematics for five years at Kiski, a prep school for boys in Saltsburg, Pennsylvania. Then, having saved enough money to support himself in idleness for a year or two, he had come to Columbia to earn a degree in higher mathematics. A droning professor in the theory of differential equations had rudely changed his mind. Following a week of extreme boredom, B. gave up and on impulse dropped in at the graduate English office to ask if he might arrange a transfer. The interview with Professor Wright was dispiriting.

"Will you take me in?" B. asked. "I've had no preparation whatever, nothing beyond one term in college of freshman English."

"It would be a sinful waste of time," Professor Wright said.

"I'd like to make up for my lack of education," B said.

"A little late in life to begin. But—well, I suppose you can try."

15

We worked in my room at night while B. read doggedly on, from *Beowulf* to *Adam Bede,* from Michael Wigglesworth to *Daisy Miller.* Too often I sat at my desk typing master's theses with two carbons on some depressing subject like biochemistry or political science. The few hundred dollars I had saved for graduate school were nearly gone; I could pick up extra money this way. Three mornings a week I worked as a typist for the Home Study Department of Columbia, a busy correspondence school offering college courses by mail. If I was unwilling to take B. for my husband, I was equally unwilling to let him pay my way or support me.

"It has to be fifty-fifty," I told him.

"Why not?" he said. "I'll tell you how good a feminist I am. You can pay for us both if it makes you happy."

B.'s mind was sound and adjustable—an uncommon man. One of his ancestors was named Reason Bevington; perhaps that accounted for it. He passed brilliantly with a "first" when we took our examinations for the master's degree, and his thesis on Matthew Arnold pleased his advisor, Emery Neff. I had my thesis yet to write. Before the June commencement, on the night of May 20 when Lindbergh was flying the Atlantic, we went to a midtown speakeasy to celebrate this glorious victory over ignorance. The address was a brownstone mansion on Fifty-second Street, where we groped down a dark flight of steps to the basement entrance and knocked at the armored door. Cautiously a small panel slid open and from behind an iron grille a single cold eye stared out at us.

"Hello, Joe," B. said bravely. He drew from his wallet one of his modest collection of speakeasy cards and held it up for inspection. "Mr. Salvatore Antenucci sent me," B. said. The Antenuccis kept a greengrocery on Amsterdam Avenue, a friendly Italian couple who made a fuss over young lovers like us. Mrs. Antenucci had already explained to me the secret of cooking good spaghetti. "Use plenty of erl, you know what I mean?" she said.

Immediately the panel slid shut, the speakeasy door was unbarred. A courteous Italian proprietor ushered us into one of a series of small dining rooms, lavishly decorated in red plush with heavy curtains to shroud the windows. The tables stood close together, the lights were low, the air was intimate, the place stirred with warmth and laughter. It felt exclusive, like joining the Athenæum Club. Who minded breaking the law of the land?

We sat holding hands across the table, after ordering scallopini and a large, costly bottle of Chianti. The wine when it came astonished me. For the first time in my life I tasted something alcoholic that tasted good, unlike the bootleg whiskey or Prohibition gin at college dances, the hooch, the pure alcohol flavored with orange pop, the raw Dago red. After a while we became tipsy, and it felt wonderful, wonderful.

"Mein Herz, mein Lieb, meine Helena," murmured B., holding up his glass.

I stared at him in a daze of love. "How perfectly you speak Italian," I said, sipping the red wine.

*

I asked my boss, Mr. Langston, to hire B. for the summer in the Home Study Department, and there we worked full-time to remain in New York together. B. moved into my rooming house, with a room he seldom occupied, directly beneath me on the second floor. He became a "field representative" for Home Study, traveling over Brooklyn and the Bronx to ring doorbells of prospective students snared by Columbia's advertising. When he signed a customer for a Home Study course in Biblical Literature, Boy Scouting, Fire Insurance, Slide Rule, or the Contemporary Novel, his commission was fifty dollars. Though successful at it, he hated this role of high-pressure salesman, tracking down a poor store clerk or naïve housewife to peddle a little learning, signing up the misguided and the innocent.

Yet it was a splendid summer, a long and happy summer of love. We read a travel book, Konrad Bercovici's *Around the World in New York,* that showed us how to circle the globe on the weekends. New York *was* the world, where one read *The World* newspaper each morning. By following Bercovici chapter by chapter, we explored the distant shores of the metropolis—Syria, by taking the subway to Rector Street, walking a block west to where Syrian rug dealers squatted before their shops and Syrian coffeehouses contained men smoking narghiles.

We went to the Russian Bear on Second Avenue to drink tea and hear the balalaika, to the German-American Athletic Club on Third Avenue to drink beer and eat knackwurst. We found Italy on Mulberry Street among the pushcarts and incense-laden Catholic churches. On the lower East Side we chased after gypsies—Russian, Romanian, Hungarian gypsies—because Bercovici was lyrical about them.

But on the night of August 22, we went nowhere, an eventful journey. We sat in my room at midnight watching the clock, and like Felix Frankfurter and Heywood Broun, Edna St. Vincent Millay and other involved citizens, we wept. A shoemaker and a fish peddler were being executed in Massachusetts. For the wrongful deaths of Sacco and Vanzetti, we were bitterly ashamed and wept.

*

Then I decided I couldn't marry him or anyone at all. In the following spring I faced the miserable, terrible, unquestioned fact and ran away.

The second year of graduate school had been more incredibly happy than the first, a time of two earthshaking events—of being hopelessly in love, and of reading the entire works of Henry David Thoreau in twenty volumes. Each experience changed my life radically for the better. I sat in the library beside B. day after day that winter of our content, reading most often Thoreau's *Journal*, which occupied fourteen of the volumes, with its amazing entries that explained the principle of the good life, the doctrine of simplicity. "Do what you love," said Thoreau. "Pursue your life."

To me his words made an enormous difference, like a shining light. He had discovered a way to live that seemed a beautiful economy, reducing his wants, thriving on solitude among the bullfrogs, "no more lonely than the loon in the pond." I was reading him with extra care to write my master's essay on his ideas of nonconformity. And since B. was fully occupied with other studies, I alone became the disciple of this simplifier, this freethinker, this rash believer in freedom and the independent spirit.

When I tried to tell B. about Thoreau, I wasn't very successful. It appeared I made him sound less than irresistible, not being eloquent enough. B. observed I was the kind of reader that writers nightly pray for. He thought this another of my simple transports, like the earlier one for Edna St. Vincent Millay. He was skeptical that Thoreau had any gospel of reform whereby to illuminate and shake the world.

"But he says, Simplify, simplify!" I cried. "He believes in living abundantly the simple life."

"He's hardly the first, is he?"

"But how fierce he was in going his own way to find it! He refused to conform. He demanded a life that was free. He fell in love with a shrub oak. When he went to the woods and lived by himself among the otters and woodchucks and listened to the hoot owls, he wrote in his journal, 'Are not these advantages?'"

"My God," B. said. "That's because he didn't have a girl."

By February I had finished my thesis on Thoreau's remedy for civilization and submitted it as the final requirement for my master's degree. On February 7, B. celebrated the anniversary of our falling in love by buying me a diamond ring. That morning in class I reminded him of Donne's poem "The Anniversarie"—"This is the second of our raigne." And he remembered the magnificent words from the same poem:

> *Who is so safe as wee? where none can doe*
> *Treason to us, except one of us two.*

In my room that night he tried to lead up to the matter of slipping the ring on my finger, but the scene wouldn't arrange itself.

"I want to give you something because I love you," he said. "Guess what it is. Three guesses."

"A lemon ice-cream soda," I said.

"Try to keep your mind on the subject," B. said. "Close your eyes and concentrate. What is it I want to give you?"

I closed my eyes. "A lemon ice-cream soda with lemon ice cream in it," I said. "Come on, let's go to the drugstore and get one."

I jumped up to put on my coat. B. rose and jerked it away from me, pushing me back savagely on the daybed.

"Goddamn it, Helen!" he shouted. "This is the most exalted moment of my life. Will you shut up about lemon sodas?"

He drew a tiny jeweler's box from his pocket and showed me the small solitaire inside.

"It's a diamond," I said.

"Do you like it?"

"Oh, sure, I love it. I *love* it! It's beautiful. But it's an engagement ring. Isn't it an engagement ring?"

"Don't you want to be engaged to me?"

"No."

We sat without looking at each other, in bleak and silent misery. Finally he took my right hand and slipped the ring on my finger. He kissed me. "You see?" he said. "No harm done. It's only a gift. We aren't engaged at all."

*

Thoreau had taught me this—you must learn to heed your own heart. Before the spring recess in March, I decided abruptly to make an end of it, to leave him. I would go first to my mother's house in the upstate town of Hornell, New York. I packed my books and few possessions in the wardrobe trunk that stood in one corner of my room, arranged for the trunk to be shipped home, handed in my key to the landlady, and moved out. I had already secretly resigned my job at Home Study.

When B. took me to the train that morning with my small suitcase, he had no idea I was running away. But I was. And since I had run away before in my life out of panic fear, I suppose fear had something to do with it. I was afraid of being caught, losing myself before I found out who or what I was.

At the Erie Station we began wildly kissing each other goodby even before the train was announced. I told myself I would never see his face again. The only fair thing to do was to disappear, go to another city leaving no address. He deserved someone who would love him enough to be his wife. At the thought the tears rained down my face.

"I love you," I said. "I won't say anything more. Yes, I will—world without end, I love you."

Quite as griefstricken at the idea of being separated for one week, B. offered to jump on the train and come along.

"No," I sobbed.

"Telephone me the second you arrive."

"My mother hasn't a phone."

"Send a telegram then."

"No. No! *No!* I can't. I'm only going home, only three hundred miles."

"Write then! Promise me on your heart you'll write to-night."

"I'll write and tell you everything."

*

My mother lived alone in a house on Maple Street, a lonely, deeply unhappy woman. Her marriage to my father Charley had ended in divorce when I was two years old. Now twenty years later she had not remarried or found any solution to her life. She merely existed alone, with almost no friends and no diversions. She worked for the Erie Railroad in Hornell as a clerk typing paychecks in the Accounting Bureau, and her life appeared to me unbelievably dull and wretched. I could never understand how she put up with it, the endless monotone of days at a desk, with nothing but an empty house to come home to. She read no books, only the evening newspaper. She kept no garden. She went nowhere except occasionally on Sunday to visit her two aged aunts, Aunt Net and Aunt Lydia, who lived a few streets away. My mother stayed alone and slept alone, but her life was not in the least free and solitary like Thoreau's. It seemed to me not worth living.

The real reason I couldn't marry—a reason I hadn't the courage to admit—was that she didn't want me to. She expected me to live with her, repay her for my life and education by rescuing her from her loneliness. My conscience, when I examined it, told me her claim was just. As the dutiful daughter she should have had, I ought to be willing to work and take care of her. I felt an overwhelming sense of guilt. She had refused to remarry for my sake. What right had I to marry anyone?

"You're pale as a ghost, you look worn out," my mother said that night, as she always said when we met again.

"After you graduate this June, I want you to come home and *stay*. You're all I have in the world. You need me to look after you. I've always said New York is no decent place for a young girl."

"But, Mother, I'm not young any more. I'm nearly twenty-two. What can I do in Hornell?"

"You can teach in the high school. That's what I trained you to be, a teacher. That's what my money went for. Now you've got a good education, you can't throw it away. It's about time you made use of it."

"I'm going to pay you back every cent," I said.

"You'll pay me back by coming home, being my daughter again. You've been away at school six years. I've hardly seen you in all that time, summers and all. Believe me, it's been no picnic living day and night alone."

"I'll take you to Chicago," I said. "We'll go there to live, the two of us, and I'll get a job to support you. I planned the whole thing out today on the train. Just give me a day or two, a little more time—"

"Chi*cago*?" she cried in bewilderment. "You mean where your *father* is? You must be out of your mind! Why should I give up a good job to live in Chicago, of all places? You mean to be near your *father*? Well, no thank you. I'll stay where I am."

"All right, Boston then," I said desperately. "Philadelphia. Tulsa. Salt Lake City. What does it matter? They always need teachers somewhere. I can't talk about it tonight but, oh, trust me. I promise to look after you for the rest of your life. We'll be together. I *promise* you."

"I'll believe it when it happens," she said. And we went off that night to the movies.

*

I spent the next three days writing a farewell letter to B. that would explain everything. I had to convince him how final it was—my mother's need of me, my determination not to marry, my sense of utterly inescapable fate. We could never meet again. He must understand and find someone else. He must let me go.

Before I could send it, a telegram arrived from B. saying, "Whats wrong am going absolutely nuts I love you," followed by a special delivery letter in the same tone. He had gone to my apartment with the idea of writing me from our room, and Pauline had let him in. There was the room empty of anything of mine.

"Helen moved out," Pauline told him. "Didn't you know?"

In alarm he raced over to the Home Study office, bursting in on the secretary, Miss Lindsay.

"Did you two have a quarrel or something?" she asked. "Helen's gone."

"Maybe it makes some kind of sense," B. wrote. "But for Christ's sake, tell me so!"

I went back that afternoon to my letter. It must be mailed quickly now. I sat struggling with the final draft, writing, crossing out, rewriting, staring blindly into space. It was like a suicide note. How did one say so simple a thing that would destroy one's whole life? The doorbell rang. I didn't answer it. After a number of persistent rings I put down my work, wiped my eyes, and went to the door.

"I've come to get you," said B. on the doorstep. He laughed and took me in his arms.

"When I love anybody, it is for life," he said, among other things. "Do you know who wrote that?"

"No."

"That poor old spinster Horace Walpole."

*

We were married the first of June. My mother demanded of us that much delay, hoping I would come to my senses and change my mind. She wrote me daily letters to New

24

ry us. Dottie was there, my college roommate who had
eed on a week's notice to be my bridesmaid, and Paul
lley, B.'s friend from the Kiski school. The two of them
d met that morning in front of our rooming house and
t sight had fallen in love. They were gazing hotly into
ch other's eyes, useless as attendants, paying no heed to
he rest of us.

I saw my mother's accusing face and I grew hysterical,
suddenly sick. I turned to B. close beside me. "I can't go
through with it," I whispered. "I'm so sorry. I'm sorry for
this incredible mistake. It's my fault. I should have known.
You'll have to let me go!"

In panic I half rose from my chair, preparing to run out
of the place and keep on running. Only my mother was
watching us. B. gripped my arm and held me down.

"No, you don't," he said fiercely in my ear. "You can't
go! Haven't you found that out yet? You belong to *me*, not
to her."

We had invited nobody to the ceremony. Our friends
around Columbia invited themselves and came anyway.
The Antenuccis came, bringing a bottle of red wine. Doris
and Pauline came (Rita had married her lover Carlos and
was living in the Bronx), even Mr. Webb, the professional
bridge player. The Home Study Department shut down
for the afternoon, and the whole staff nearly filled the
Chapel. They had chipped in and bought us a floor lamp.

It was an honest-to-God wedding after all.

York outlining my folly. When I re
a few days at the end of May, she con
confirmed her anguish by making m
though I wanted no wedding at all.

The dress was pale-pink chiffon, sty
with a short skirt, to wear with a fetching
net trimmed with pink roses over the righ
the dress as it was, stained by my mother's
after work at night painfully stitching it.
put her head down and wept with deep wren
hated her martyrdom, her despair, her tears, an
dress that caused them. I hated the idea that a p
ask so much of one's life. On the last evening t
her grief drove me to the frantic extreme of ma
promises.

"I'll marry him for one year," I said. "Be patie
me that much happiness. Then I swear, I *promise* t
I'll come back to you."

"What do you mean by that?" she asked.

"I'll get a divorce," I said.

It made her furious to hear me lie. "Oh, yes," she s
with contempt, "I can see you doing a thing like that f
me."

In childhood my mother had made me a promise, often
repeated: it was that some day I would understand. But understand what? Her life? My life? Even then it had sounded
more like a threat: some day I would grow up to recognize
her pain and my own ingratitude. And now the time had
come, and there was nothing that I could understand.

B. and I were married in St. Paul's Chapel at Columbia
on a Friday afternoon. At the luncheon beforehand, in
something called the Golden Glow tearoom, I could look at
nothing but my mother's tragic face. She sat dumb with re-
buke opposite me, next to B.'s father, a Methodist minister
in Ohio who had come with his wife, B.'s stepmother, to

2

"Marriage is a great improver," wrote Jane Austen, who never tried it. We went to live in Greenwich Village, not in a garret but in a shabby old redbrick, two-story house off Sheridan Square at 139 Washington Place. Before the wedding we had sublet the whole second floor—two tiny furnished rooms and bath—from Margaret Marshall, literary critic of *The Nation,* and her husband, Hal White. Hal was a poet whose verses seemed to appear mainly in *The Nation,* but for a livelihood he taught English at New York University in Washington Square. They sailed for Europe for the summer the day we moved in.

We had rented the place in the evening, when to our bedazzled eyes it looked bohemian and beautiful, far more alluring than by the cold light of day. There was a little chintz, a charming picture by Wanda Gág. But the kitchen had no sink. And the bathroom, at the head of the stairs, was painted a blinding electric blue. The living room with two wicker chairs, scarred china closet, and gateleg table, looked out on a popular cabaret or night club upstairs across the narrow street. B. and I slept on the folding couch under the open window and made love each night to the craziest jazz and the noisiest whooping it up in the Village.

And, oh my, we loved it, we didn't mind at all. We had a colored maid named Ophelia who came once a week to clean and left the flat a little grubbier than before. We had both our names printed large on the mailbox, which pleased B. to appear to be living in sin like a true Village pair. Mine came first, then his, since from the start I insisted on keeping my own name.

I wanted to preserve my identity, in marriage not in bondage, whatever that meant. Smith was anonymous enough. There were about three thousand Smiths in the New York telephone directory (a figure I read somewhere) and, until we eventually got a telephone, no Bevingtons at all. Yet it seemed necessary to hold on to what I had. I kept my maiden name—like Margaret Marshall and Heywood Broun's wife, Ruth Hale, and lots of women in the 1920's—because I was a Lucy Stoner at heart, determined to be counted and free. It didn't mean I had a personal quarrel with society or felt obliged to hold feminist views. B. was always a better feminist than I. He believed in the right of women to be equal or even superior to men, self-supporting to boot if they wanted it that way. I was more in favor of being a person, or perhaps merely of being myself.

In the same spirit of independence I tried to hold on to my money and my books. By marrying I hadn't promised to give up anything. When B. decided to construct a bookcase of a few boards and old bricks, I told him to make two bookcases, one for either side of the doorway in the living room. The left would be his, the right mine. We would sign our own names in our books and keep them separate. This plan worked perfectly till the following day when we stopped at Schulte's Fourth Avenue bookshop and bought a secondhand leather-bound copy of *La Chanson de Roland*. When we got the pretty volume home, there was nowhere to put it on our shelves.

"May I have it?" I asked B. in doubt. "Or shall I give it to you?"

"It's ours," B. said.

We put it on the table.

I told him, "We're still fifty-fifty." We weren't—not for a moment, not where money was concerned. In the matter of income this remained strictly his world. Ten days after marriage I started looking for a job, and on that same Monday morning B. went to work by being called for by a liveried chauffeur and driven in a Rolls-Royce out to a wealthy estate on Long Island. "Work" he laughingly, and I ruefully, called it.

Through the Placement Office at Columbia, B. was hired for the summer by a millionaire cracker manufacturer, Mr. Hooker, to tutor his twelve-year-old son Dale and prepare him for Andover in the fall. I think Mr. Hooker also made pretzels and soda biscuits. He lived in a garish, half-timbered mansion on a pretentious landscaped estate on the Sound with a private beach three hundred yards long, and his wife was a peroxide blonde who drank beer for breakfast. Mr. Hooker drank whiskey steadily after 4:00 P.M., a silent, morose man who took no vacations. B. spent five days a week and one evening as Dale's companion, teaching him a little Latin and algebra, playing golf with him and tennis, swimming, racing in the motorboat, sailing on the Sound. Once a week they were brought into New York in the Rolls-Royce or the Cadillac to have dinner at the St.

Regis and attend the theater or a concert together. Dale was a lonely, negative boy, fond of B. But, damn Mrs. Hooker, she was fonder still. She flirted with her son's tutor, giving out scandalous hints from time to time about needing a little private tutoring herself.

B. came home each night exhausted from so much lying in the sun. It was amazing how the life became him, how handsome he looked with a deep coat of tan. His muscles ached from playing games all day and handling boats. Dressed in striped flannels or plus fours, he had just had two Scotch highballs on the patio with Kitty (Mrs. Hooker), who said his teeth thrilled her. They were the whitest she personally had ever seen.

"And what have you been doing all day, darling?" he inquired.

My first interview was with Ginn and Company. It sounded vaguely like the kind of work I wanted, in a book-publishing house, and the sternfaced woman who talked with me thought I might fit into a place. Then she looked down at the ring on my left hand.

"Are you by any chance married?" she asked. "I understood you to say you were *Miss* Smith."

"Yes, I am married."

She froze at the word. "In that case, I'm afraid we aren't interested," she said, dismissing me. "We have a strict rule against hiring married women. If you don't mind my asking, why don't you stay home and have babies?"

After that I left my wedding ring behind. My next interview was on West Fifteenth Street with Margaret Sanger, who five years before had opened in Manhattan the first permanent birth-control clinic, even inventing the phrase birth control. This time it might have been tactful to wear my wedding ring. But I excused myself anyway from her offer to take me on trial. Much as I admired her, she seemed too intense, too dedicated to the crusade—a reformer who had been arrested eight times and gone to prison to further the sexual freedom of women. I was afraid she might want me to sell copies of the *Birth Control Review* on Macy's corner at Thirty-fourth Street.

I went to work instead for Miss Mary Smalley, editor of the *Journal of Biological Chemistry,* over by the East River in the buildings of the Cornell Medical School. It was a seamy district of tenements and poverty, far removed from the luxurious green estates of Long Island. On entering the building of a morning, I would step over the body of a drunken woman sprawled across the steps. Or I gave my lunch, carried in a paper bag, to a hungry crying child.

Yet the job had virtue, being in general all it should be. Miss Smalley, redhaired and uncertain of temper, a meticulous spinster who loved detail, taught me many things I wanted to know. I learned nothing of the polypeptides, amoebicides, and esters about which I read manuscripts all day long. But I learned proofreading, and a great respect for the splendid structure of the English sentence. I learned to hate dangling participles and split infinitives, to which the scientists were fiercely, immovably addicted.

There was time for reading books on the slow streetcar ride crosstown to and from the office—for colossal works like *War and Peace* and *The Decline and Fall of the Roman Empire.* They accompanied me like bodyguards. And I carried in my pocket long lists of German vocabulary to learn at lunchtime. I was young and untutored enough to believe that what knowledge went into the head would forever stay put, turning at last into wisdom. One had only to go on living to fill the mind to overflowing.

*

The Village we lived in was a magic place—not what it had been in its heyday, of course, when Edna St. Vincent Millay flourished there. I never actually met a poet in its bookshops, not even the bum Joe Gould. No radical like John Reed, no rebel like Floyd Dell showed his defiant face. Yet the bloom remained. It was a real village, simple and relaxed, with a more than common informality, a carefree air. A few consciously eccentric characters still walked the streets in smocks or togas. It had too many quaint little cafés and tearooms, like The Mad Hatter, The Pig 'n' Whistle, The Pepper Pot; too many antique-jewelry shops; too much batik. But there were always the narrow twisted lanes and the Italian pushcarts and the friendly people—a tolerant, easygoing village. I think nothing on earth looked sunnier than Washington Square of a Sunday morning, after a late breakfast in some arty tearoom run by a former wife of Hendrik Willem Van Loon.

Our main social event of the summer was a huge cocktail party on Long Island given by the Hookers. I wore the pink chiffon wedding dress, B. his navy-blue wedding suit, and we went out by train, the earliest guests to arrive by more than an hour. Only Mr. Hooker was in evidence on the patio, a bottle of Scotch at his elbow. From his cold, brooding silence I gathered he hadn't wanted us hirelings invited. It was his wife's doing, as the wild Saturday-night party was her idea, and the crowd when it appeared consisted of a hundred bored and insolent guests, hangers-on and parasites, some of them complete strangers, who came to drink themselves sodden and pass out on the Hookers' liquor.

Mrs. Hooker wore a Hawaiian number splashed with crimson flowers, a floral arrangement in her brassy hair. I was prepared to hate her on sight, but how could I? I didn't hate her, even when she kissed B. and greeted me by saying, "I simply adore your cute little husband, honey. I hope you don't mind sharing him with little old Kitty."

In the midst of the drunken party, where nobody had a face, I would hear Mrs. Hooker's insistent voice, shrill and off-key, repeating the same words like a theme song: "I scrubbed floors for Hooker, yes I did. I got down on my hands and knees when we were poor and I scrubbed his dirty floors. And, oh God, I was so happy, I was so happy." Tears streaked her mascara and fell on her rouged cheeks. "Then he made all that goddamned money."

On the train home at midnight, B. said, "You're the lucky one. At least you needn't apologize for the way you earn your living."

*

It was still July when disaster struck. B. never went back to Long Island and the Hookers again. A few nights after the party he threatened all at once to die in my arms, before we had begun to learn how to live. Apparently the trouble came from a sharp blow on his shin one day in the motorboat. The sickness developed fast, sudden and extreme, a return of the osteomyelitis that years before, at the age of fourteen, had attacked the marrowbone of his left leg and nearly killed him.

As the infection spread deep into the bone, B.'s temperature shot up to 105 degrees and he became delirious, crazy with pain. On that horrible night, before I got him somehow into a taxi (not knowing how to summon an ambulance), up the few blocks to Orthopaedic Hospital, where the bone surgeon Dr. Farrell operated to relieve the pressure, drain the pus, and save him from a general septicemia —on that night I think I experienced the ultimate in pure stark terror.

During those fearful, endless hours, I discovered two things that shook me and I found amazing to believe—that what I wanted above all else in this perishable world was to have a child of B.'s. And that the only way I knew to solace him in his agony was to read him a book.

Frantic with unendurable pain, B. lay on the bed and held on to me with both arms, from time to time clutching

3 3

my throat and staring demented into my eyes. "Read, *read!*" he cried hoarsely. "Why are you silent? Why don't you *read?*" But I was already reading. In the nightmare I had reached out as for heaven's help to pick up the first book at hand—the most placid of Trollope's Barsetshire novels, *Doctor Thorne*. Afterwards I could never bear to look at its tranquil pages again.

*

B. was ill four months, well into November, unable to return to classes in the graduate school at Columbia or seek a teaching appointment in the New York area. He got about on crutches by day and worried by night over our rapidly dwindling finances. He swore that the cabaret band across the street played only one number till dawn—"I Can't Give You Anything but Love, Baby."

When Margaret Marshall and Hal White returned from Europe in September, we moved a block away to Van Nest Place, to a rented furnished room in the third-floor apartment of a young working couple named Schiller. To move one Sunday morning, we borrowed a pushcart from a friendly Italian and piled into it our worldly possessions: the brass floor lamp given us by the Home Study Department, our clothes and books, a few bricks to start a couple more bookcases. I pushed the pushcart while B. hobbled alongside on crutches.

It took us a week to realize the strangely ominous nature of the house on Van Nest Place. Since our room looked out on the street, we missed the fact that the backyard, enclosed by high brick walls, contained four large, vicious German police dogs. We failed to notice that no name appeared on the mailboxes in the downstairs hall except the Schillers' and our own. Or that when a long black car regularly sped up the street and stopped at our door, several furtive men emerged and slipped into the house, men who wore dark suits and black fedora hats pulled down over their eyes. The hats made us wonder in the end. We spoke to Mrs. Schiller.

"Who are those characters downstairs, anyway?"

"I hate to tell you!" she said quickly. "The whole outfit is a gang called the Vitelli brothers. They own this building. Their families occupy the first two floors. Fred and I never lay eyes on them, and they won't ever bother you. But it's sort of creepy, you know? It gets me sort of nervous. They've got this still down in the basement, a whiskey still, can you feature that? And those killer dogs out back! You know what they are? Sure you do. They're *bootleggers*."

We knew the name, Vitelli. They were notorious enough, bootleggers and whatever else—gangsters, mobsters, racketeers, gunmen. They handled both wine and hard liquor, Mrs. Schiller said, and they distilled the liquor in the basement.

This was bad, admittedly this was bad. We couldn't tell the police, of course, who would do nothing; we would only be murdered for our pains by our landlords. We felt uneasy most of all about the danger of fire, since the stairway walls were redhot to the touch as you climbed to the third floor. I would put out my hand and shudder. At the same time I breathed in the comforting smells of Italian cooking. So we stayed on for five months, more or less poised for flight, not once meeting a Vitelli brother face to face or any of his family or gunmen. It was healthier to believe they didn't exist.

In November when Al Smith, wearing a brown derby, chewing a cigar, and yelling "Baloney!," ran against Herbert Hoover, I voted for the first time in my life—not for the Democrats like B. (I couldn't stomach them), but a straight Socialist ticket. Norman Thomas had sat opposite me in the subway one day when we both got on at Columbia at 116th Street, and he had smiled benignly in my direction. Al Smith was a bad loser, Hoover a bad winner. Norman Thomas was an uplifter. He was my man.

B. went to work for the B. F. Goodrich Company as a sales representative in their New York office, selling rubber goods (except contraceptives) about the time that Professor Saidla telephoned to ask if he would teach college English three nights a week at Brooklyn Polytechnic. If someone had suggested he conduct Sunday excursions to Coney Island, he would have done that too.

Our salad days were here again. We began to make money fast, with the extra advantage so useful in married life of having no leisure to spend it. We came and went, more than ever in love but hardly on speaking terms with no time to talk. After Christmas I started teaching, as I had always expected to do. I answered an advertisement in the *World* for a female high-school teacher, no details given, and after a brief interview found myself hired at the Bedford Academy in Brooklyn. It was a private school with classes from kindergarten to teachers' training, run by the two elderly Victorian Miss Moshers, who paid me one hundred dollars a month to teach everything in sight—high-school English, European and American history, civics, biology, astronomy— six classes before lunch and a survey of world literature after in the teachers' training school. B. said I was being exploited as slave labor, but the truth is I still owe the old girls money for the chance to learn how to teach.

Miss Smalley allowed me to leave the *Journal of Biological Chemistry* on short notice, admitting sadly she had hoped I would be content to stay and take over the editorship on her retirement—presumably in about twenty-five years. Out of affection and deep gratitude, I confessed as I left to being a married woman, a fact that stunned her. But I kept the secret well hidden from my new employers, the

36

upright Misses Mosher, though it grew increasingly hard to remember to leave my wedding ring at home, more and more ridiculous to play the innocent role of Miss Smith.

To teach, however, was the work to which the Lord had called me, what I was born and bred to do. I had put off my lifework too long.

"You know, I'm really a born teacher," I said to B. after the first day's classes. "I'm in my element. Aren't you?"

"How can you tell so soon?"

"I like the sound of my own voice."

*

We tired of eating Village tearoom food and living in the ever-present threat of being raided by the Revenue agents or caught in a crossfire of submachine guns in the downstairs hall. In February, 1929, we moved to a three-room apartment in Long Island City and furnished it ourselves. Paul Culley, who had stood up with us at our wedding, came from Princeton for a visit and gazed around at the transformation—the brand-new possessions, the easy chairs, the upholstered sofa, the coffee table, the gray woolen rug, particularly the ruby-red Shantung curtains I had made for the windows. Paul couldn't help laughing.

"So you've settled down at last," he said mockingly. "The two radicals, the two bohemians, living it up in the Village. Now look—an old married suburban couple with an icebox and a double bed. I knew you'd give in and turn respectable, Mrs. Bevington."

It was an attack on all that Thoreau and I stood for— Thoreau who said always to travel light. He wasn't a collector, he was a rejecter, of possessions. With a sweep of the hand I disposed of any question of their permanent value.

"You're wrong, my dear. We'd sell every piece of it, every stick of furniture tomorrow. Wouldn't we, B.? It means nothing, *nothing,* all this. We can walk out any time and leave it behind. We're still free."

Paul laughed and so did B. That was in February. Four months later, in June, we sold the entire contents of the three little rooms, all but the red silk curtains, the books, and the floor lamp from Home Study, and took a trip around the world.

*

B. had the idea of going to England for a few weeks in the summer. When he casually mentioned it, I gasped in unbelief, speechless at so rash an undertaking. Then I said, "Can we afford to go?"

"No, I suppose not. But we might make it one way."

That was enough for me. Next day after school I hurried to the Placement Office at Columbia to ask for another job to fill in the vacant hour before supper. In that gracious time of plenty, those abundant pre-Depression days, work existed for the asking—typing a thesis, reading a manuscript of some aspiring writer willing to pay a dollar an hour to have his grammar and syntax straightened out, tutoring a dull student, teaching English to a foreigner.

Thus I met my splendid friend Nikolai Vassilieve. I still thank God for the accident that brought me in mid-February knocking timidly at his door. Vassilieve was a White Russian, an exile and refugee, who lived alone in a gloomy rooming house on West Sixty-sixth Street, in a high-ceilinged room that contained his table and drawing board (he was a master architect with a Wall Street firm), two straight chairs, and a large four-poster bed covered with a bright-pink cotton bedspread. That was all.

I taught him the English language three afternoons a week from five to six o'clock at his figure of two dollars an hour because, as he said, teaching him English was twice as hard as teaching anyone else. Besides, he had plenty of money and he was a generous man. For four months I taught him and he taught me. I wish I could honestly believe we came out even. Vassilieve freely gave me instruction in the art of living, of the kind Thoreau had given—with a few extra hints thrown in on the virtue of being born a Russian with a Russian soul and how to pronounce words like borsch and Turgenev and Anna Karenina.

My method of instructing him was a simple one, simply arrived at by Vassilieve's fierce rejection of any other possible approach. Having reached the age of fifty-two and lost most of his hair, he considered it too late to master the conjugation of verbs or memorize the parts of speech. He merely wanted to talk. And so he began in broken but eloquent English and kept on talking steadily for four months, while I made him say each sentence twice, once in his own highly original way and once in mine. We spoke his autobiography together, and the terrors of it gained by repetition. Sometimes the drama of his life grew so absorbing I would hold my breath and forget to correct him. At that he would stop and smile, wagging his finger at me.

"Ah, Miss Smith, please to remember. I am pupil, no? You are bossy, yes? Is that it, bossy? Ah ha, yes. You are the boss, remember."

Vassilieve had lived through the Russian Revolution and escaped by way of the Crimea, but by suffering he escaped, starving and almost naked. I have known a few heroic people in my time, and he was one of the brave. Having lost everything once—his country, his home, his beloved Persian wife—he felt no need to acquire possessions to lose a second time. He had become a simple man from being a complex one. He had lost his pride and most of his desires, his religion as well, and what remained was only kindness. What he had kept was charity. Anything he acquired he chose to give away. At Easter, for example, he gave me a pound of beluga caviar, a deluge of caviar, of which he bought altogether twenty pounds for his friends, though he no longer had a taste for it himself. Bread and cheese suited his appetite better.

The people he constantly helped were White Russian refugees, at this time in New York in large numbers, whom he fed, clothed, and found work for, usually as doormen or waitresses. If they needed a bed, he brought them home to share his own. One thin old man stayed for a while who had been sleeping nights on a bench in Central Park. One sullen young girl lived with him for two weeks and throughout each lesson sat on his bed and studied me with narrowed, accusing eyes. Vassilieve, facing me at the table with his back to her, winked broadly.

"I tell her you are my great teacher, my professor. You teach me English speaking. She don't like that. She—how you say?—she smells a fish. She don't believe me."

"Why not?" I asked.

"She say great professor in Russia is always man. You should be a man."

"Tell her I'm married," I said.

*

When B. and I had saved about fifteen hundred dollars, I went shopping one Saturday morning at the tourist agencies for a summer passage to England. My first stop was at the office of the NYK Japanese steamship line.

"Can you tell me please how to go around the world?" I asked the clerk nervously. "And how much it costs?"

He told me in plain terms. It was a cheaper journey than I had dreamed. First you got yourself across the Atlantic Ocean (by your own means) to Naples. You sailed from Naples on a Japanese ship, the *Haruna Maru,* say, and after five weeks on the Mediterranean, Indian Ocean, and China Sea reached the port of Kobe in Japan. You took another ship, the *Tenyo Maru,* perhaps, from Yokohama, and crossed the Pacific Ocean to Los Angeles. There you were, only three thousand miles from home, practically around the world. A ticket on the NYK Line, for two people from Naples to Los Angeles, cost $964. Except for crossing one whole ocean, half of Europe, and the entire U.S.A., it covered everything. It made the world available, fawning at our feet. If I had had the cash with me, I would have bought passage on the spot.

When I carried the delirious news home, beside myself with joy and a sense of accomplishment, B. turned red in the face, staring at me aghast. Then he had a fit. To my intense dismay, he was thoroughly angry, and the more he listened to this global enterprise the angrier he got. The worst he could say for such a crowning folly was that it sounded typically tourist-American. This may have been our first quarrel.

"All you want to do is race around the world like a damned rabbit!" he shouted. "At top speed, seeing nothing, hurrah, boys, and here we go! You won't have time to *stop* anywhere. You won't know where you've been. You won't *see* anything but a lot of water."

"I like water," I shouted back.

"Why?"

"It keeps butter cool."

Gradually after a week or two his resistance lessened, but only, I think, because he grew fascinated by the mathematics of it, trying to prove the sheer imbecility of undertaking to go so far on so little money. As a problem it turned out to be, to his complete satisfaction, insoluble. With all his calculations, B. could never bring us back nearer than California.

"So you'll have to stay on the West Coast and live," he said grimly, to punish me for getting him into this. I instantly agreed. Why not? We could always find work anywhere in America, the golden land, the place of limitless prosperity. We had no real reason for returning to New York, having gone around the world there already. The planet might yet offer another world or two.

3

Have I ever had such a light heart since? With one suitcase apiece and one book, the *Anthology of World Poetry*, B. and I went aboard the *Belgenland* of the Red Star Line, traveling third class when it was still properly called steerage. I don't know about the rest of the luxury liner during the five-day crossing, but our own cramped quarters were as light and airy as the New York subway. We ate steerage food at long bare wooden tables. We stayed on deck most of the time up in the bow with a wide view of the Atlantic, leaning against a winch or resting on a hatch, discovering an appetite for sea voyages and dreaming of more oceans to cross. I reminded myself to make a career of going around the world, round and round every year or so.

On the train to Paris, the wonder of it grew. It was the world and it was wonderful. Obviously one should visit

Paris as young as possible, at the age of incredulity. We came barely in the nick of time and it was done, never to be the same fresh miracle again.

From our room in the Hôtel de l'Opéra on the Rue du Helder, we set out to see Paris on foot, and like many a guileless tourist before me I praised God each night for the bidet in which to soak my weary feet. We saw the Mona Lisa, Napoleon's tomb, the gargoyles of Notre-Dame, the bookstalls along the Seine, Rodin's Thinker, and the naked girls in the Folies-Bergère. (*La folie pure,* said the program.) We ate snails. We looked Paris over from the Bois de Boulogne to the Eiffel Tower and found the view best from Montmartre—the Paris of blue roofs from the heights of Sacré-Cœur.

At four in the morning our last night there, we lingered on in Montmartre, sitting idly in a sidewalk café across from the Moulin Rouge. The music had stopped blaring, the dawn would soon come. We elected to have one last drink to Paris before walking all the way back to the hotel. B. recommended a bottle of stout.

"It's bitter," he warned me. "Strong, black, bitter stuff. You may not like it, though bitterness has virtue too, sometimes leaving the right taste in the mouth."

I took a careful sip. "Not only bitter, it's bleak," I said. But I liked it that way.

Up and down the quiet street at that hour of night, the prostitutes sought late customers among the few remaining men lounging in front of the cafés. Each whore looked a caricature of herself, overdressed, overpainted, grotesque and absurd—the strumpet look—swaying with swiveling hips past the indifferent onlookers in an exaggerated attempt to be alluring. One wore a tight purple dress with a feather boa around her neck, a *donzelle* for whom the only word was tarnished. Nobody moved, stirred to pity or lust for these daughters of joy.

I clutched B.'s arm to attract his attention. Down the street a pretty young girl came hurrying, dressed in a neat dark suit and white blouse, apparently a shopgirl or hat-check girl on her way home from work. She looked tiny and charming as she rushed along on high heels, glancing neither to the right nor left, a picture of innocent youth. Yet one worried about her. One longed to protect her from ravishment, from harm.

"She shouldn't be walking here alone among these harlots," I said to B. "What if some man follows her in the dark?"

Just then three men near us rose from their table, lurched to the sidewalk, and blocked the way as the girl approached. She stopped abruptly, teetering on her heels. They spoke to her and she turned her face towards them, laughing in their faces a gay young laugh, and with a sudden lewd gesture agreed, nodding her head. *Naturellement*. Two men took her arm, one on each side, the third followed close behind. Off they moved up the street like a small funeral procession to wherever her bedroom was.

"*Calme-toi*," said B., lifting his glass of stout.

*

At Innsbruck in the Austrian Tyrol we found the ultimate heaven we were looking for. On a July day as we came by train from Zurich, the Alps took on such unbearable grandeur, such incredible heights of blinding snow, that, when the train slowed down to enter an Alpine town, B. and I cried out together, "This is it! Let's get off here!" We had no idea where we were, only that it was heaven. There was no need to go further. Our ticket said Innsbruck, but Innsbruck could wait. In haste we grabbed our suitcases and leaped from the train before the conductor could stop us. Standing triumphantly on the platform, we stared over our heads at the station sign—Innsbruck.

It was while walking there with B. on Marie-Theresien-Strasse that the answer came to me where I wanted to spend the rest of my life. Up to now whenever we played this childish game, the choice had always been Times Square.

"I want to spend a year in Paris," I said, "then come to the Tyrol and live out my days in that chalet—see it up there?—perched on yonder Alp. How does that suit you, darling?"

"It suits me to a t," B. said. "One blissful year with you, clinging to a frozen Alp in yonder chalet. Then I want to spend the rest of my life in Paris."

*

I close my eyes, seeing Florence that first time, and all I remember is the statue of Michelangelo's *David*. No wonder, since it stands in three different spots in Florence—the gigantic original in the gallery of the Accademia; the marble copy, human and gleaming, in the Piazza della Signoria; the bronze copy overlooking the city to the hills of Tuscany beyond from the Piazzale Michelangelo.

In Florence I made up my mind to have a son like the heroic shepherd boy David. When I announced this decision to B., he laughed and led me to the statue of another giant-killer nearby—Savonarola, grim, fanatical, forbidding, and to the spot in the Piazza where the martyr monk was hanged from a gibbet while a bonfire flamed beneath him.

"Beware of teasing Allah for a son," he said.

Soon we were on our way to Rome in a third-class carriage, and the temperature rose to 95 degrees and we were locked out of the dining car. A fat man opposite us, weighing three hundred pounds and sweating like an ox, wiped his face repeatedly as he leaned over to shout at us, *"Il vino è buono e fa caldo in Italia!"*

"Is he telling us it's *cold?*" I cried.

"He says the wine is good and it's damned hot in Italy," said B., nodding his head. And that was the way it was.

Everywhere in Rome were the encounters—with St. Peter's foot in the Cathedral, his bronze right foot worn shapeless by the kisses of the faithful. With silver moonlight in the Colosseum. With young Keats and Shelley in the Protestant Cemetery. With the gay passing crowds on the Via Veneto. At the Hotel Roma our bed was so wide I could take a siesta lying across it without bending my knees. Even so, I had nightmares each night from the haunting spectacle of too many Romes, the smothering layers of history for the last three thousand years—ancient Rome, Christian Rome, Medieval Rome, Renaissance Rome, Garibaldi's Rome, Victor Emmanuel's Rome, and on top of the heap Mussolini's Rome, filled with frightening signs of the new conqueror: the black shirts and strutting, arrogant *carabinieri* in a city of priests and nuns. "God has been restored to Italy," announced Pope Pius XI in the confident summer of 1929, "and Italy has been restored to God." God had come to terms with Il Duce.

B. had feared we wouldn't see enough of the world on this journey. After a week in Rome he was content to go aboard the *Haruna Maru* at Naples on a hot morning in mid-July and stare at Vesuvius from the deck rail without having to climb to the top of one more Object of Interest.

*

She was a tiny ship of only 13,000 tons, now since World War II lying somewhere at the bottom of the ocean. To me she is a lost world herself, never to be found again. Twenty-three passengers were traveling second class on the *Haruna Maru*, bound for the Far East, two of them Americans, B. and I. The others were five Japanese, two Eurasians, one Hindu, one Italian, and the rest English colonials, English missionaries, one baby, and one remittance man. It was a company about the size you would expect to find in a lifeboat.

We became friends in the serene blue waters of the Mediterranean. The older of the two women missionaries, on their way to China, found a new mission in life trying to save my soul. Each morning after breakfast she stopped me on deck, took my hand in her own, gazed steadily into my eyes, and asked with deep concern, "Are you washed in the blood of the Lamb?" Each night after dinner she stood on deck looking anxiously on as I danced with various men—my husband, the Italian (who knowing no English would say politely as we danced, "I love you, I love you"), or the remittance man—and next day she hunted me up to inquire urgently, "Are you washed in the blood of the Lamb?"

"Good morning," I would reply. "How kind of you to ask."

The British tea planter, on his way to Ceylon, took B. aside and warned him about the remittance man, first explaining what that was—a man paid a remittance by his family to live out in a colony and stay permanently away from home.

"We've got one on board, you know," said the planter. "The fellow is a perfect bounder, a cad, sure to be. They always are."

"How do you know what he is?" asked B.

"By the look of him, simply unmistakable. I've run into them too often out in the East not to know the breed. Shifty, you know, can't trust them. Their own families can't abide them. If I were you, I should be very careful to keep the blighter away from your wife."

"My wife can take care of herself and of me, too," said B. "It's a talent I admire in women. That's why I married her."

"Good Lord," said the planter.

*

Actually we spent most of the time in first class, since with so few passengers the ship's officers came aft to invite us. No barriers existed between classes. The swimming pool was on the first-class deck, a square canvas bathtub that held three or four swimmers at once if nobody minded the crowding. Of a sunny afternoon, our most illustrious passenger sat nearby in her deckchair—Mrs. Woodrow Wilson, widow of the President—and presided, gracious and plump, a little queenly, dressed in flowered gowns with a matching parasol over her head. To win her smile, we dived and frolicked like porpoises, and she smiled her favor or lightly waved her handkerchief. On the ship she occupied the "Kaiser's Suite."

The finest friend we made was a major in the Egyptian army, Major Barakat, who came to our table in the first-class lounge one night while we were sampling a brandy, bowed low from the waist, presented his card, and asked B. if he might be permitted to dance with me. The music seemed appropriate to the occasion: "I Kiss Your Little Hand, Madame." The Major had the most flawless manners of anyone I had met in my life.

By the time the ship reached Port Said at the entrance to the Suez Canal, we were such good friends that the Major invited us to Cairo to visit in his home for a month or two. When we reluctantly refused, deciding to continue the journey on the *Haruna Maru,* he made a second proposal which we accepted.

As the ship docked at six that morning, we left it in the gracious company of Major Barakat, preparing to travel by train to Cairo, almost 150 miles away, spend the day there, and return by rail the same distance to Suez (the two sides of a triangle), where we would meet our ship as it arrived about midnight at the other end of the Canal. Several other passengers, including Mrs. Woodrow Wilson, were doing the same thing. They were being taken to Cairo on a Cook's Guided Tour, while we were honored guests of the Major.

At the end of the three-hour journey, the Major's car and his chauffeur waited for us. He had telegraphed ahead to tell his wife he would be delayed till night in arriving home. After six months away in Europe, this amiable man chose to spend the hottest day in July sightseeing in Cairo, unaware that we should have preferred to visit his home and meet his family. All morning we sped from mosque to museum, from palace to citadel, with the Major a relentless guide, leaping into his car and out of it as he gave crisp orders to his chauffeur to drive on to still another shrine or monument. We stood with him on the sun-parched banks of the Nile and solemnly promised to return.

After lunch at the hour of siesta, the Major did what no self-respecting Egyptian would do in the suffocating heat of the day—took us out to the Pyramids of Giza. In burning sun and blistering sands on the edge of the desert, we tramped for hours, staring with sun-blinded eyes at the Great Pyramid, considering the riddle of the flat-faced Sphinx. The Major, a swarthy, stout man close to middle age, found the extreme heat overpowering. With the utmost gallantry he bore it, making one concession to comfort—to escape the blaze of the sun he spread a large white handkerchief over his balding head and set his red fez on top, so that he looked like an Eastern bride, with a veil hiding his face from view except when he lifted the veil and peeped out and with a slight shudder dropped it again.

We cooled off at a luxurious dinner at Shepheard's Hotel, and the twilight came. Our train for Suez left at eight o'clock. The last act of generosity by Major Barakat was to buy me a huge box of baklava at a pastry shop and for B. a tin of Egyptian cigarettes. At the station he bent low over my hand in farewell. "I Kiss Your Little Hand, Madame."

When we stepped from the train at Suez, more than three hours later, it was eleven-thirty. The few passengers, all Egyptian, hurried past us into the night, and we stood alone on a deserted station platform.

"Where's the Canal?" I asked B. apprehensively. It must be somewhere in sight, yet we stared about us helpless in the dark. We could see nothing.

B. went in search of a porter to ask directions and if possible hire a taxi. He returned to say there was absolutely no one about, not a living soul. Suddenly there was some-one. Out of the shadows a man crept and approached us. Even in the dark I could see that he was unwashed, his white robe dirty and bedraggled, his manner sly and cringing. He had a fat paunch, and in his red fez and black drooping mustaches he looked murderous.

"Help you, lady? Gentleman? You need dragoman, need guide? I speak seven languages including the American. Where you want to go?"

"Don't *tell* him, B.!" I cried out. "Don't speak to him!" I turned in fright and ran down the platform, B. chasing after, and behind him the dragoman.

"Maybe he can help us," B. said, catching up. "It's nearly midnight. We're in trouble. We've got to do something *fast*."

Hurriedly he began to explain our plight to the drago-man, who grasped the story before he heard it. He took us in immediate charge.

"No canal in Suez, no canal here," he said with a shrug, spreading his arms to include the entire city. "See? No boats, nothing here." Of course I knew better than that; he had to be lying. It was, wasn't it, the *Suez* Canal?

"Where is the bloody thing?" asked B.

"Canal at Port Tewfik. That's oh, two, three mile from here. All right, gentleman, I take you. We get a car and I take you. You leave it to me."

"He's going to rob and murder us!" I whispered to B. in anguish.

"No, lady. No, please, Madame," said the dragoman, overhearing. His voice whined and he wheedled. He held out his hands in an imploring gesture. "I got wife and ten children, lady. All I want is earning a little money. I get you to ship, you pay me not much, only fair. You trust me, lady."

We had to trust him, it seemed. In the ancient, ramshackle car that he produced with alarming haste, we went bouncing out of Suez into the flat countryside. An evil-looking driver came with the car to whom the dragoman spoke in Arabic, then turned to give us the answers.

"All right, now I tell you. Ship she is coming later, not here yet. Sometime ship take long while coming in line through Canal, very slow. One hundred miles through Canal. We find Cook's Tour people. You know Cook's Tour? They wait for same ship like you."

"Cook's Tour!" we cried in rapture. Why had we forgotten about them? "Where *are* they?"

The dragoman shrugged, waving his hand vaguely back the way we had come. "Somewhere. In Suez, in hotel, maybe? Maybe took different train? Driver he don't know but he say agent expecting them. We find them all right. This only road going to Port Tewfik, see? They got to come this way sometime."

We drove for several miles, careering through the midnight countryside under a brilliant fullface moon—till with a slamming on of brakes the driver jerked the car to a stop, the dragoman motioned us to get out. B. and I stood uncertainly in the dirt road, staring around perplexed for the Canal. Where were we? No Canal was here, nothing, no water, no harbor, not a ship or a house in sight—nothing but a high wooden fence extending along one side of the empty road.

Without warning, the driver abruptly started up the car

and roared away toward Suez. In amazement we watched him go, then looked to the dragoman, who taking us each by the hand led us across the road through an open gate in the high fence. There we emerged into a railway yard with a small railroad station next to the tracks. Our guide stopped before a wooden bench outside the station, groaned heavily, and sat down to rest, motioning us to sit beside him. The place was in deep shadows, completely deserted.

"What in the name of God is going on here!" yelled B., losing his temper at last. "Why have you brought us to this godforsaken place? Where is the *Canal?* What the devil does this mean?"

The dragoman smiled up at him. "We wait here for Cook's people," he said.

"What do you mean *here?* I want you to take us to the Canal, don't you understand? The Suez *Canal!* To our ship! It's very late, we must hurry! We've got to find our ship!"

"No, gentleman, sorry, can't do that," said the dragoman. "We got to protect the lady. This good hiding place, we wait here for Cook's people. They come by and by. Down by harbor we can't go, no, that *much* too dangerous for lady, she not safe by harbor in the night." His hands reached like claws toward our throats to demonstrate the danger. "Port Tewfik bad place, bad men on waterfront, they murder you, they steal, they hurt, they kill. No, gentleman, we stay here."

For the next couple of hours we sat on the bench beside him, not talking, listening for a car to pass on the road. Not a single car passed. The night was beautiful, warm, silent, calm, the road moonlit as broad day. But not a car passed.

About two o'clock in the morning, the dragoman rose and stiffly stretched. "I take a leak," he said and disappeared. In anxious whispers B. and I considered the fix we were in. Our ship might already have come and gone, with the

Cook's Tour on it, leaving us behind. We wondered whether to make a desperate run for the Canal—wherever it was.

"He's out there to meet an accomplice," I said. I didn't trust the dragoman at all. He skulked. He smelled bad. I took off my diamond ring and hid it in B.'s breast pocket. "They'll be back in a minute to rob and murder us."

"Sh-h-h-h!" B. whispered. In the road outside the wooden enclosure, a few feet away, a man stood motionless listening to us. He looked ghostly and unreal in the moonlight, dressed in long white flowing garments and an Arabian head-dress, carrying a tall staff or shepherd's crook. In the white road he seemed an Old Testament figure emerged from the past. Then he moved forward and entered the enclosure, and I saw his black-bearded face and fierce eyes. And I screamed!

At that moment the dragoman appeared. The stranger rushed furiously with uplifted arm to strike him and spoke in a perfect torrent of words. Both men shouted at once, gesticulating, more and more excited. The dragoman whined, he cowered. The stranger raged at him, violently angry. Several times he pointed to us with his crook, and once he strode over majestically to the bench to stare down at me. I hid my face in terror in B.'s arms.

"He Arab, speak no English," explained the dragoman in deep gasps, when he had a chance. "I been telling him about you. He terrible *angry,* oh my, he want to beat me! He say we shouldn't be here. He say we make bad trouble for him. Now he got to stay with us all rest of the night."

"Why?" asked B.

"Because of lady here. He Arab policeman, carry no gun only stick. He say lady not safe in Port Tewfik, like I told you. She in great danger of her life. He say he got to watch lady all night and try to get her safe on boat."

I looked up at the stranger for confirmation of these words. His face was stern and dark, his black eyes flashed with a towering fury.

We relaxed a little after that and sat back to gaze at the stars and listen for the sound of a car passing on the dirt road. The Arab stood guard over us, tall and inscrutable, darkly brooding. And slowly, slowly, the night wore itself away.

Towards dawn I began to feel sorry for the weary drago-man, who groaned to himself, perhaps at the thought of his wife and ten children in their beds in Suez. I unwrapped my box of baklava and offered him some—offered some to the Arab policeman, who lifted his head in disdain and re-fused to notice my gesture. We smoked a few Egyptian cigarettes, B. and the dragoman and I, and devoured the honeysweet baklava, even laughing a little together as the white light of morning began to fill the sky.

Finally, at a curt signal from the Arab, we rose and marched out of the railway enclosure. Four abreast, in stride, we walked swiftly up the road towards the harbor, and soon we could see the glittering Canal in the distance. On reach-ing it, we turned along the quay, where a few sinister types lounged at the waterside, and kept walking till the Arab found what he sought—the launch that now at dawn waited at a landing place to take us to the *Haruna Maru* somewhere out there in the harbor.

I offered the Arab policeman my hand in grateful fare-well, and with a smile he courteously bowed and took it. His eyes were no longer angry. B. offered the dragoman all the money he had with him, enough to let a man sleep in his bed for a week. We were ready to go aboard the launch, when the last act of the drama brilliantly unfolded—the Cook's Tour people drew up with a flourish in the same old brokendown car that had taken us out of Suez, Mrs. Wood-row Wilson and the frazzled rest. The whole unlikely story had been true. They had spent a wretched night in the lobby of a Suez hotel, waiting for news of the delayed *Haruna Maru*, and they were vexed and bored with the tiresome adventure. B. and I were not bored. We had survived the night's search and found the Suez Canal at last.

*

When I feel unbearably hot, I remember the Red Sea. In that narrow strip between Arabia and Egypt, we sailed into a red furnace and for four days to the Indian Ocean stifled from the heat. The British colonials in pith helmets retreated under the canvas awnings to drink whiskey punch, assuring us of sudden death from heatstroke if we stepped out in the noonday sun. At night B. and I carried our mattresses to the deck and slept there, and even the stars were scorching hot and beautiful.

After turning the corner at Aden into the Indian Ocean, we felt the relief of fresh winds, until we noticed the fevered activity of the sailors closing portholes, battening down everything loose, removing awnings and last of all the deck-chairs where we sat. Headwinds were blowing, the little ship pitched and tossed, in sharp gusts came the torrential rain. Rumors grew and spread uneasily, then doubt turned to certainty. We were on the edge of a typhoon.

You have to find out sometime how good a sailor you are. When the typhoon struck and we were hurled headlong into a furious cyclonic storm of lashing winds and angry seas, the question in the mind was not so much of peril as of performance: whether you could keep on your feet while others succumbed and were prostrated.

For nearly a week we endured the heavy squalls and high turbulent seas. How many mountains, how many valleys long was this journey? The tiny ship appeared stricken, emptied of passengers. To make matters worse, the stewardess followed me about. "You feel awful, Madame?" she asked, a small Japanese woman squinting up into my eyes. "I bring you little broth. You feel better to lie down."

"I feel *fine*," I said, resenting her concern. It was hard to stay upright and stagger around the wildly pitching prison with the howling of the sea wind, the steady crashing of the waves. The books I had borrowed from the ship's library made grim reading in a tempest—Conrad's *Typhoon* and a work called *Nature Notes for Ocean Voyagers*.

B. and I sat at dinner the last night in lonely splendor. We laughed with pride at our survival. Then wham! a wave crashed over the bridge, and someone had left a porthole open. We were awash, the water pouring in gallons over our heads, dashing our meal to the floor, all but drowning us. Nothing worse happened. The whirlwinds gradually lessened, we emerged next day into bright sunshine and calm waters. The virtue of the storm was this—we had stayed on our feet. As the saying is, we kept the forked end down. We were seaworthy. That was worth taking a journey to find out.

*

Ceylon rose up an enchanted island from the sea. On shore in the port city of Colombo we rode in rickshas and visited elephant shops to buy a gold, ivory, ebony, satinwood, or cocoanut-carved elephant, not buying one in the end. Who wants an elephant on his hands? The streets were crowded with Tamils and Singhalese, though it was the exquisite Tamils, the south Indians, who really belonged there with a physical beauty fit for Ceylon. They were so slim and dark and handsome, with long black hair, luminous eyes, straight noses, and red lips, that it wasn't easy to tell male from female. They had been made equally lovely by a benevolent Hindu god.

I studied them for a day or two and said to B., "Don't you think this is the right place to spend the rest of our life?"

"If we had a life to spare," he said.

But it was so suitable. We rode to Kandy seventy miles

away in a hired car with a Dutch honeymoon couple from the ship, who knew as much English as we knew Dutch, not a word. On the mountain road were green groves alive with monkeys, here and there a banyan tree. At Kandy the Buddhist temples stood alight with priests in saffron robes chewing betel nuts. The Dutch couple clutching a bottle of Hollands gin only added charm to the excursion, being unstinting with offers of gin, speechless in our language, smitten by love, and like us extremely fond of elephants. Each time we met one wallowing along the road, twenty times, they stopped the car and tumbled out to snap its docile picture. Ceylon still makes me think wistfully of elephants and love.

Yet we hadn't seen the last of the Tamils. Sixty of them came aboard the *Haruna Maru* as deck passengers and from Colombo to Singapore lived their languid, graceful lives under our eyes. The indolent women in white saris lay back on pallets while the men did the housework, cooking the rice on tiny braziers and feeding it tenderly to their wives. Behind a partition an Untouchable cooked his rice and ate meditating alone. On the rail above their heads, which was lined with spectators day and night, we leaned to gaze down at them spread over the lower deck, like figures from the pages of the *Ramayana*.

*

In spite of the stinks of Singapore, compounded of mysterious spices, sewage, and dead cats, I wept in grief that the world was so small. And life so short. We were already halfway round, past many splendors, on our way home. What I really wanted was to spend the rest of my life aboard the *Haruna Maru*.

Before Hong Kong on the China coast, it became clear to me that the remittance man was a British spy. Colonel Morrison, about thirty years old, wore a monocle and an insolent stare. His words were clipped and strangely guarded; he kept severely to himself, ill-mannered, overbearing, rude to everyone. When he appeared on deck, he took pains to snub me, passing B. with a curt nod. Yet after dinner he would ask me to dance, or rather sweep me out on the dance floor. The man was provoking and uncivil. We learned nothing whatever about him—who he was, what he was, or where he was going.

As we approached the fortified harbor of Hong Kong, Colonel Morrison became very secretive and he took endless pictures. He concealed himself furtively in odd corners, but then he was always furtive and inscrutable. His behavior grew more erratic at Shanghai, where because of a cholera epidemic we were forbidden to leave the ship. Colonel Morrison raised a terrific row, storming about, arrogantly demanding to be put ashore. A few hours after docking in the muddy Whangpoo River filled with junks and sampans, the captain changed his mind and permitted only Colonel Morrison to disembark, and he fled down the gangplank shunning everyone. Later the captain let the rest of us go at our own risk. Three or four passengers left the ship.

B. and I spent the day in Shanghai in the eclectic company of a gentle Japanese scholar who had attended the University of Michigan. He had a high Oriental giggle, one of the weird sounds of this earth, but he didn't laugh long. Believing his life in peril, he blanched with fear and his voice quaked. "They hate us!" he whispered over and over, staring in horror about him; "They *hate* us!" pointing on every side to the flaming banners, reading aloud the taunting slogans, "Drive out the foreign devils!," that named and included us all.

Twice on the Nanking Road rocks came hurtling into our hired car, thrown not by boys but by angry men, and our companion shrank back in his seat trembling like a child (who at home taught philosophy and, presumably, the existence of good and evil). We were unhurt, but it was an appalling day. The one peaceful sight was the Lunghwa Pagoda; and later Colonel Morrison showed me a snapshot he had taken of it.

*

I didn't want to spend the rest of my life in China or Japan either, for different reasons. Japan was too contradictory, too unreal. The NYK Line paid our train ticket across Japan from Kobe to Yokohama, and we took two weeks for the journey. To our intense alarm, to our speechless dismay, Colonel Morrison followed us off the boat at Kobe.

"Shall we join forces in Japan?" he murmured behind his hand, as if slipping a message to a fellow secret agent. "I'll meet you at the barrier."

"Shake him!" B. told me furiously. But how could I? We lingered on saying goodby to old friends of five weeks; to Dr. Kubo, the ship's doctor, who gave us letters to Japanese hotels in Kyoto, Tokyo, and Yokohama, praising us as famous American educators and very meek people.

So we walked mourning away from the *Haruna Maru,* a world loved and forever lost, with only Colonel Morrison glued to our side. "Righto! March! Our first stop is Nara," he said briskly, and meek as mice we followed him through customs to the railroad station. At the station bar he ordered an absinthe, not inviting us to join him. Since we had never tasted absinthe or supposed it obtainable, we ordered it too— a heavy dose of wormwood fumed with licorice, so strong one might take it with an eyedropper on the tongue. But what kind of man drank *absinthe* at nine o'clock in the morning?

Nara, forty miles away, proved that the liquor had gone to my head. It seemed inhabited entirely by deer, parades of tame deer roaming the streets, wandering freely as cats—

a majestic buck by himself or groups of does and young fawns. With them the unreality of Nara was complete. Do travelers fail to bring back news of such miracles, or does one not listen? Who, after all, keeps a secondhand memory of a place? Nara was an oasis of peace, hushed and holy, meant for the contemplation of Buddha in the midst of herds of sacred deer. When we bought rice cakes from a vendor to feed them, the fawns ate from our hands, nosing us like puppies, licking our faces. We stood braced for the rush of the greedy antlered buck deer, leaping and bounding under the ancient oaks.

Colonel Morrison promptly acquired a new personality at Nara, and by lunchtime I loathed him. He could be obnoxious so variously, a deplorable man. In the role now of military expert and martinet he stormed the place, menacing with his camera, pointing it like a pistol at man and deer alike, snapping us to attention and ordering us (his troops) from temple to shrine. At the Temple of Todai-ji, a colossal bronze Buddha more than fifty feet high sat in the middle of a lotus flower regarding his insolent sneer as he took its picture, its face expressing forgiveness and utter peace. At lunchtime, our leader refused permission to pause for lunch.

"Don't be absurd!" he snorted when I said I was hungry. "How like a woman!"

"But I *am* hungry."

"What of it? We have no time to waste watching you eat." He consulted his guidebook and with a bark of command led on.

I tried munching a rice cake but gave up and handed it over to the nearest deer. In exasperation I turned to Colonel Morrison, squinting coldly at me through his monocle.

"You remind me painfully of someone, and all day I've been wondering who," I said. "Now I know. It's Napoleon."

We three stayed the night at Kyoto at the Torii Hotel. Next morning at breakfast the proprietor stood before B. and me sighing deeply, shrugging his bent shoulders in apology. Our friend, he told us in pidgin English, had left at dawn in a great hurry after arguing over the bill. He had given us the slip. He had slapped us in the face. He had gone without goodby, unbewailed, unmissed. But travelers must be content.

"Thank God, we've lost old Mata Hari," I said to B.

"Old Captain or Colonel or Knight in arms," he laughed in relief.

"Not velly nice man," observed our gentle host, to comfort us for the loss.

*

Tokyo was most contradictory of all. The delicate toylike paper houses looked too destructible, the floating lotus blossoms in Ueno Park, the fragile doll-like women walking in the Ginza under bamboo parasols, too unequal to life in the teeming city, one of scars and rubble left from the frightful earthquake. Tokyo everywhere denied its fragile beauty with ugliness. Or was it ugliness only softened a little by beauty?

After a week of sightseeing, B. took me to a final showplace. Late one afternoon we went by streetcar to the Yoshiwara, a licensed quarter for prostitution, where we might compare the whores of Tokyo with the bawds of Paris and New York. The same contradiction existed in that distracting, opposite place: it was at once ugly and patently beautiful.

As sunset we strolled like lovers through the six main streets with the one entrance gate—another Eden, was it, with no forbidden fruit, or only a prison enclosed by the police? Innocence or sin, was it, grace or blemish? At that serene hour the ladies of the quarter were out strolling arm in arm, their faces heavily enameled and expressionless, their black hair lacquered and ornate, their vivid kimonos circled by a rich silk obi. They looked not wanton but as conventionally Japanese as a print of Mount Fujiyama. Fragile, courteous, unreal ladies, they moved with tiny steps and gently swaying bodies, making their procession, while from nearby came the delicate soft strumming of a samisen.

We lingered on, enchanted, wandering past rows of graceful little houses with pretty bamboo fences in front, past more ornamental dwellings with yellow chrysanthemum gardens and groves of cherry trees. In a ticket office of one house, a buxom ticket-taker sat smiling with a baby at her breast.

From time to time B. was winsomely beckoned to with soft glances from the hospitable doorways, and I looked with interest to see if he meant to leave me to sit patiently on the front steps of some flower-trellised cottage and guard his shoes. Each time he pointed with regret to me tagging along beside him, sighed and shook his head, and we laughed and walked on.

*

Before the *Tenyo Maru* sailed from Yokohama, B. bought me a Japanese kimono. We had the address of an exporter and easily found the shop, where we stood for a moment gazing at the exotic wares in the shop window. A customer inside the door was holding to the light a crimson silk kimono, squinting haughtily at it through his monocle, haggling with the clerk over the price.

For twenty minutes after we entered the little shop, we waited for Colonel Morrison to finish making a scene. During his loud transactions, a master of slights and slurs, he disdainfully bought *three* kimonos (for a harem?) and by his

63

crushing manner and withering look nearly reduced the male clerk to tears. If the colonel saw us a few feet away throughout this performance, he gave no sign. At last he picked up his box and with relentless incivility, without even a sideward glance, strode to the door.

It was too much. "Colonel Morrison!" I called after him. "If the time has come for us to part, old friend, I want you to know how heartbroken I am to say goodby."

He turned without a start of recognition and gave me one last quizzical, contemptuous stare. *"Sayonara!"* he said and kicking open the door dashed out of our lives, the most odious man I have ever met, one not attuned to the human race. Perhaps he really was a remittance man.

*

I don't know how tempting the Pacific might have looked had we seen it first, not last. By now we were growing world-weary. Besides, as B. had predicted, we had run out of money. We were flat broke.

The ocean stretched too wide, the week on the crowded *Tenyo Maru* too long, broken by a stop in Honolulu to eat the fresh Dole pineapple (the only thing we could afford to eat), and marvel at the vulgarity of the hula. On the last night before San Francisco, the ship's officers invited us to a small party to help drink the liquor on board before it was locked away and sealed when we entered the twelve-mile limit of American Prohibition waters. The joyous party went far to cement the affection between two nations—a feeling we grieved to remember later on the day of Pearl Harbor.

"Those gentlemen are now my *enemy?*" B. asked in sad incredulity.

We stumbled down the gangplank at San Francisco into my mother's waiting arms. She had traveled across the country to meet us at the boat. And we were red-eyed and blear, reeking of whiskey, with almost three dollars left in our pockets—an embarrassing state of affairs that we felt obliged to hide from her as best we could. My mother's sharp eyes didn't need to count our money. She observed how frayed we were, how shabby, in need of haircuts and having our shoes resoled. While B. looked for a taxi, she began to sum up the situation.

"I'm afraid you've married a tippler," she said. "Your husband has a very peculiar smell."

B. faced our financial state with enterprise and forbearance. Not once did he say "I told you so." I had to say it for him: "We're in a pickle, aren't we?" Instead of our staying on the *Tenyo Maru* as we might have done with passage paid to Los Angeles, he registered us at the sumptuous Palace Hotel and took my mother to dinner that night where he could sign for the check. He then sent a telegram to two maiden aunts in Cleveland ("Go to the aunt, thou sluggard") to ask for the loan of five hundred dollars. Without reproach they saved our lives—two prudent old ladies who spent their own lives teaching school for a total period, between them, of one hundred years, yet never once did they throw their money around by taking a trip to Europe.

During the three days before the *Tenyo Maru* departed for its last port, B. dutifully hunted for work in the San Francisco area, being interviewed by the heads of two junior colleges and a dean of the University at Berkeley. It was already September; they cordially invited him to join the faculty next year, a mere twelve months from now. Meanwhile I entertained my mother by taking her on free sightseeing trips as the guests of realtors determined to sell us real estate in Palo Alto or Menlo Park.

Then B. and I thankfully fled to our ship to sail down the fogbound coast to Los Angeles, and my mother followed along by train. There was no question about it, California was not the promised land. It wasn't even America, B. said

65

cheerfully. We would have to return to New York where we belonged, back where we came from.

Someone told us if we could find a corpse to accompany we might travel by railroad on a free ticket. This proved a forlorn hope, no body presented itself, though by coincidence in Albuquerque a man approached us in Fred Harvey's restaurant to ask if we would care to take charge of a dead uncle on his way to Chicago. By then we had bought a one-way excursion ticket to New York on the Sante Fe and were riding in the daycoach with no stopovers. Impatient at such beggarly performance, my mother had given us up and taken a Pullman to visit the Grand Canyon.

B. and I arrived in New York on an autumn day late in September, 1929. It was exactly one month before the Crash —when prosperity collapsed and ended in America, when sudden panic, hysteria, and the failure of the stock market ushered in the fearful beginning of a new era: the terrible Depression. A decade had closed in earthquake, in catastrophe. The boom was over. A world had come to an end. For the first time in our young lives, we realized this was something a world could actually disastrously do—it could fail. It could be undone.

Yet to us the gods were ironically kind. We had no money to our name and therefore nothing to worry about, no savings, not a stock or investment, not a cent in the bank or out of it. We had nothing at all to lose.

4

Being penniless didn't bother B., not especially. Nor was he frightened by this new turn of events. Nothing threatens a man who doesn't feel threatened. Of the two possible views of existence, the light and the dark, he chose the first, an optimist with his own talent for living in the light. He used to quote something to me during that calamitous season from James Stephens' *The Crock of Gold* —something about its being wisdom to go through life without fear, not to be hungry in a hungry hour. B. was saying it nearly four years before Franklin D. Roosevelt got around to.

On October 24 when the panic started, Black Thursday, we were back at Columbia University, living in an apartment off Broadway on 122nd Street. Our three rooms had a simplicity Thoreau might have envied, with a borrowed cot to sleep on, a borrowed card table to eat on, and two wooden orange crates to sit on. For a touch of elegance there were the brass floor lamp from Home Study and the red curtains at the windows. We had no telephone, radio, or refrigerator, but we had several hundred books stacked on the floor. We lived next door to a garage, and our holy and impeccable neighbors were the Jewish Theological Seminary, the Union Theological Seminary, and Dr. Harry Emerson Fosdick's Riverside Church.

We had hurried home to Columbia to enroll again as graduate students, working together for the doctor's degree. To pay the tuition required money—three hundred dollars —which we borrowed from the University. At that blithe and happy moment of penury, I suppose our future was in the greatest possible peril. Black clouds hung thundering over us, a precipice yawned at our feet, yet we saw nothing but the usual fair skies. We leaned on hope, expecting to go on living by our wits, not knowing that the market for wits had already crashed too.

Neither of us had any employment, and very soon there would be no employment anywhere to be had. In the grim Depression just beginning, we might have been lucky to peddle vacuum cleaners from door to door. We might have joined the breadlines or sold apples on the street corner to survive. Or we might not have survived at all.

But the gods chose to let us off. B. and I walked across campus that autumn morning—after signing a note putting us now eight hundred dollars in debt—without a worry in the world, more utterly in love than ever, delighted to be students again. We heard someone shouting our name and turned to see Miss Barnes of the Placement Office racing across the grass towards us, waving her arms.

"Do you want a job?" she yelled to B.

He laughed and met her as she came up panting. "Sure," he said, "if it isn't in the state of California."

"It's at New York University in the Bronx," she said.

"They called me on the telephone only a minute ago, and I happened to look out the window and saw you passing by. 'Wait!' I said, 'I think I have the man for you,' and dropped the phone and ran. They want an instructor in English, starting immediately. Can I send you up for an interview today?"

If B. was going to teach, I thought to myself, then I would have to teach also. That afternoon I telephoned the Misses Mosher, my old employers at Bedford Academy, Brooklyn, whose telegram had been forwarded from our last address in Long Island City inviting me to return to them this fall. Classes had begun, said the younger Miss Mosher over the phone, but they were shorthanded. She promptly offered to make me head of the English Department in the high school, at one hundred dollars a month for eight months, the same fat salary as before.

"I have to tell you first that I'm married," I said. "My name is changed—it's Bevington now."

There was a brief pause for consultation at the other end. "We are happy to hear it," Miss Mosher said stoutly. "We'll expect you on Monday, Mrs. Bevington."

At that instant Miss Smith, who had hovered like a jealous ghost over my life, disappeared forever from the scene. It cost me fifty cents to have my name changed on the records at Columbia, which on thinking it over I decided was worth the price.

"Life," the poet Cummings inquired of it,

dost Thou contain a marvel than
this death named Smith less strange?

B. made me feel like him a millionaire, rich and secure even in these hard times. They came to be known as the desperate years, the anxious years, the downhill years of the Depression—shameful years for the jobless, the needy, the dispossessed, the hungry, for people on relief, defeated and hopeless. They were bad for millionaires too, who lost their shirts as well as their private yachts, railroad cars, Newport estates, polo ponies, and giltedged securities. The dictionary says, *depression*. See *sadness*. Yet to me they were in many ways the happiest years of my life. And they grew steadily in grace. One never knows, Thoreau once said, in what hour his life may come.

New York University saved B. from disaster and allowed him to keep his pride. It was almost the only college in the country that refused to reduce salaries or drop any of its faculty to join the ranks of the millions of unemployed. His small salary as instructor remained frozen for the duration, but it kept on coming.

In our working lives, B. and I saw little of each other, only at breakfast and supper, in bed, and in the classroom. We enrolled for an evening class at Columbia in Anglo-Saxon with Professor Cabell Greet. (A couplet of John Crowe Ransom's always puts me in mind of Anglo-Saxon:

No belly and no bowels,
Only consonants and vowels.

Mostly consonants.) Never good at languages, I found it the deadest tongue of all. The temptation was great to spend the hour in the old fashion, writing lovesick notes to B., offering him quotations on the frailties of love, or making grocery lists on the margin of my notebook. "It is a bawdy planet," I would begin as the class got under way. *"La vie est vaine: un peu d'amour—"* But B. had stopped fooling. He replied to such frivolity in capital letters: REMEMBER NICHOLAS MURRAY BUTLER, who was supposed to have mastered Anglo-Saxon in two weeks.

On Saturday mornings at 9:20, we sat side by side to hear Professor Fletcher's lectures in the Renaissance, a course that started with Dante in the thirteenth century (Fletcher was a lover and translator of Dante) and lingered on in the fires of Hell so long that we barely passed through the flames of Purgatory to catch a glimpse of Paradise, let alone the Renaissance that flowered in England more than two centuries later. Yet the course had merit. It made me a hell-gazer for life, with a great and abiding taste for hell and its topography—from Homer's to Dante's to Milton's to T. S. Eliot's—where I've felt thoroughly at home in darkness visible ever since.

Our other Saturday-morning class, by all odds the winner, was in the History of the English Language with Professor George Philip Krapp. The pleasure here resided in the man himself. I wondered then about my teachers, as I wonder still, which of them deserved the honorable name, who among them really taught. For one thing, a true teacher is never dull. What he has to say takes on the rapt air of Keats looking into Homer.

Like Marcus Aurelius I learned strange wisdom from my instructors. To heaven it was due, he said, that he had known Apollonius, Rusticus, and Maximus. From Apollonius he learned to bear grief; from Rusticus to write in plain Latin; from Maximus to love mercy and exercise self-control (Maximus, who never needed to correct himself because he never went astray).

Professor Krapp was one of the passionate, undaunted few, and two others in my life were Thoreau and the Russian refugee Nikolai Vassilieve. They had something in common—simplicity, perhaps, or at least a simple belief in the merit of their calling. They taught the art of living (and the language for it), and in the midst of teaching they revealed themselves. Later I found the same quality in Montaigne (too ill-taught, he said, to teach others; yet he asked the question "What do I know?"), and in Gilbert White of Selborne (who like Montaigne sought to find the answer)—each gained the mastery of himself. Each spoke

7 1

fearlessly in his own person, and it was the revelation of a man.

*

An early effect of the Depression was to make us veer to the left—I mean the Left. Any school child could see that the political and economic structure of America needed rescue from collapse, a better sharing of this world's goods. If Hoover was a helpless President; if cheeseparing Calvin Coolidge observed dryly from retirement: "When more and more people are thrown out of work, unemployment results"; if the Mayor of New York, wisecracking Jimmy Walker, capered heedlessly in the nightclubs, a dapper and corrupt playboy—what about Karl Marx? Doggedly I read *Das Kapital,* without the light of understanding. In the end what I felt towards dialectical materialism and the rise of the proletariat was a little yearning and a lot of ignorant good will.

B. and I went to Socialist meetings, to a big Socialist rally in November where the speakers were Heywood Broun, John Dewey, Rabbi Stephen Wise, and my old friend Norman Thomas—all mild, amiable liberals whose enlightened views would frighten nobody. They were about as revolutionary as a string quartet. Far more lively and entertaining, I thought, was Heywood Broun's rally for the unemployed, where lovely Helen Morgan draped herself on top of a piano and pined for Bill, "He's just my Bill, an ordinary guy," till your heart would break, or sang huskily,

> *Some day he'll come along,*
> *The man I love . . .*

Mae West strutted across the stage in white mink, all hot, pink-spangled flesh, gold hair, and diamonds, looking like a well-kept, well-heeled madam not in the least unemployed. "Why doncha come up an' see me some time?" she drawled in her bedroom voice, batting her eyes and wiggling her torso. It was Diamond Lil inviting every customer to take heart and be a man again.

But for radical ideas I preferred Bertrand Russell and the coming Social Revolution, as revealed in his new book *Marriage and Morals*. "A trumpery book," B. called it, being fond of the word trumpery. He read it to please me and scoffed with amusement.

"It isn't that I object to adultery, not at all," B. said, "only to the idea of its being compulsory."

We went to hear Bertrand Russell speak in Town Hall in debate with John Cowper Powys on the question "Is Modern Marriage a Failure?" Yes, indeed it was, Mr. Russell assured us, winning each round by shattering argument and logical proof. While he demolished the institution, I sat on the edge of my seat, wholly persuaded he was right, and B. lay back in sleepy boredom, regarding both Russell and me with lackluster eye.

"Never mind, love," I told B., "it isn't *our* marriage they're talking about." Ours wasn't a modern marriage. It was everlasting.

*

Slowly we prospered, paid our debts, and acquired possessions—the bare necessities of life like a bed, dishes from Macy's, and a six-volume edition of Boswell's *Life of Samuel Johnson*. To these we added a single extravagance, one luxury, a real splash. In the spring of 1930 we bought a little secondhand Whippet to the tune of seventy-five dollars from our friend S. Stowater, a graduate student at Columbia, who for the price of the car threw in driving lessons. B. had never owned anything before but a horse.

Our friend S. Stowater refused for years to tell us what the S. stood for, a blight on his life. When Sto was born on a farm somewhere in the West, his fairminded parents refused to give him a name, fearing to burden him with the wrong one. Boy, they called him, till in time he could freely choose a handle of his own. Then one unhappy day when he was six and started to school, the teacher giving him a hard look asked, "What's your name?" Terrified, he stared at her and opened his mouth to report.

"Seattle," he said.

We kept the Whippet parked on the street in front of our apartment house, gazing down on it with love, breathing it in like brandy from our windows on the third floor. Goldplated though it looked, it was a rusty black two-seater, high and erect, with a square top, dog seat, and running boards. In June we planned to drive it the three hundred miles to my mother's house in Hornell. We had been married, unbelievably, two years—so long I couldn't recall my maiden days. What did we do until we met? *Were we not weaned till then?* John Donne asked the same question.

"Do you enjoy being married?" I inquired of B. on our second anniversary, giving him every chance to put his heart into it and weigh the profit and the loss. Since he happened to be reading Chaucer, Chaucer was what he quoted:

Non other lyf, seyde he, is worth a bene,
For wedlok is so esy and so clene.

Which nobody can deny.

We needed a summer holiday. Five days a week I took the hour's journey by subway during the rush hour to Brooklyn, preparing my lessons while hanging on to a strap in a suffocatingly crowded car, being pushed, squeezed, shoved, cuddled, and pinched from behind by my fellow man. I learned by necessity how to read a page once and know what it said, long enough to teach its import that morning. As head of the English Department, I carried a dead fish or frog in my pocket to dissect in biology class, or a fresh egg to demonstrate to my students the beauty of osmosis.

B. went by subway in the opposite direction to University Heights, returning home at night covered with chalkdust. He had a great appetite for chalk, a relish for teaching the bright Jewish boys who made up most of the student body. Though I was eager to become a faculty wife, whatever that might be, nobody came to call or asked me to join anything. The city life we led in three boroughs—Brooklyn, Manhattan, the Bronx—meant three separate areas of existence, none of them touching the other. But so long as B. came home with love in his eyes and wasn't late for supper, I didn't mind.

On the morning he passed his driver's test, we lighted out for Hornell. I had only a learner's permit and no stomach for this brash expedition, since neither of us handled a car well. To help with the driving, I read aloud every road sign and traffic regulation out of town and through the Catskills. On the open road I said once, "Look, there's a car coming! Pass it on the *right!*" at which B. became frantic and threatened to put me out of the car.

I was behind the wheel going through Liberty, New York. At a traffic light I drew up behind a motionless car and crashed into the rear bumper. It was a real jolt. "That's my girl," B. said. "That'll pin his ears back." The driver plunged forward in his seat, turned to look in stunned surprise, leaped from his car, and ran toward me with a raised fist.

"I was setting dead still, lady!" he yelled in outrage. "You saw me, not moving an inch. Just setting there!"

"I was rattled," I said.

"She was rattled," B. said, coming around to speak to him. "My wife drove up intending to stop. She cut it a little close."

"*Close?*" cried the man wildly. "Close, hell. She *hit* me!"

Unable to find a scratch on his car, the man accepted a dollar for shocked nerves. After that B. drove, and for the rest of the day I looked at my own country, Upstate New York, at the hardwood hills and green valleys, the Holstein cows, rail fences, Mail Pouch chewing tobacco advertised on weathered gray barns. And I thought of other things.

I thought of what I wanted most in my life—an inquiry begun at the University of Chicago four years before when one day, with my fortunes at their lowest ebb, it occurred to me to wonder what under the sun I wished for. Three impeccable wishes had at that empty moment descended from the sky, all of them in due time graciously granted by the ever-listening gods. I took it for signs and wonders. They were, in this order: a man, a graduate degree, and a trip around the world. Having got everything I wanted, I thought I might as well try again. Now seemed a likely moment to cast around for three more wishes, that is if my cup was not already running over, if I wasn't riding too high on a banana peel.

And yet, I realized, however worthy a thing was that one craved, the gods might nevertheless forbid it. Some wishes might appear to them too trivial, some too soaring. One had to pitch the note right, a grace note stressed lightly. In fairness one might expect a few benisons in this life to be unattainable—like a perfect body, say, and a confident mind—no matter how passionately one desired or even deserved them. The gods (or They) would send down blows or benevolences according to their will.

Also, a wisher had to help himself, not sit back and wait for mountains to move. He must not expect to see Jove's golden scales suspended in the sky for his benefit. He must not speak aloud his private yearnings but walk humbly and delicately in order to propitiate the somewhat lesser gods. This was no time for *hubris*. With these simple rules in mind, I thought hard and made three more wishes for the future, starting this summer.

First, to learn German (part of the requirement for the doctorate). To accomplish this end, we had several German grammars plus Schiller's *Maria Stuart* with us in the car.

Second, to play a decent game of tennis, so as not to disgrace B. We had brought along our rackets, which were lying behind me in the dog seat.

Third, to conceive a child.

In a way, it seemed, wishing was always circular. It was the same revolving desire for accomplishment and love, and the circles were concentric. Yet once again the gods deigned to listen, the attentive gods, generous in assent, unfailingly just and kind. To this day I can't speak a sentence of coherent German or play tennis worth a damn. These were beyond their bestowing. But the gods knew well what they could give, and they were unquestionably kind.

5

Dr. Caverly was an obstetrician with a swank office on Park Avenue. At first glance he seemed to me too modish a doctor, an attractive bachelor in his forties whose reception room was filled with fashionably dressed women, so slim, so smart, so bored that I marveled what their ailment might be. He had been recommended at the great Medical Center at Broadway and 168th Street, of which Sloane Maternity Hospital was a part. When I had gone to consult him at his office the preceding May, I had found him a charming man with easy manners and perfect understanding. I wanted to have a child, I told him at this first interview, and timidly inquired the cost. It was like asking the price of a trip around the world, cheaper than I expected. Cut-rate for students. A bargain.

"I wonder when it would be convenient for you to deliver me?"

Dr. Caverly looked startled. "Are you pregnant?" he asked.

"No."

He threw back his head and roared with laughter. "Well," he said, "I'll have to leave it up to you. We figure the date of birth about nine months from conception. You might try to avoid the national holidays."

I supposed that was the way my generation had children —when and if they wanted them, no longer by accident or entirely by the grace of God.

When we returned to New York in the Whippet in September, I was out of a job. Though the Misses Mosher had taken me to their hearts and classrooms in a married state, it was too much to ask them to take me pregnant. Millions of others in America were jobless. Unemployment went on and on, gaining momentum like a plague, and there was no end.

In the autumn of 1930, the International Apple Shippers' Association had the bright idea of selling apples to the unemployed. Overnight the city was awash with apple vendors, on sidewalks and street corners with a basket and a sign: "Unemployed. Buy an Apple, 5¢ each." Big, red, polished, shiny apples—B. and I bought them daily from the needy sellers, who acted as if we had done them a personal favor. We walked along Broadway forever munching an apple, choked by it, sick to death of eating apples. Then another shabby man in a frayed overcoat or no overcoat at all would stand shivering on the next corner, always the same hungry men with pleading eyes and the frightened women, trying to stay alive, not to starve too openly. Worst of all, they looked embarrassed at their beggary, filled with humiliation and shame. That year I lost forever my taste for apples.

The long sullen breadlines appeared now, the soup kitchens, the bums, the panhandlers, the people sleeping in subways. Plight had turned to disaster. The Depression was a fringe of heavy shadow around us, a time of want, a constant threat to our lives. Anxiety for the future gained a new intensity of meaning. These were evil days to be carrying a child.

Yet that year two improbable structures, a skyscraper and a bridge, rose to mock a city's bankruptcy: the silver span of the George Washington Bridge trembling in the wind, and the silver shaft of the Empire State Building. At 102 stories the tallest building in the world, it was the mightiest ever built by man, a shocking monument to Progress, half-empty for years.

The appalling misfortune of the many, growing steadily by the hour, was never mine. At a merciful remove, I only watched others turn pauper and starve. Through the help of a friend, Betty House, I was hired in October a few doors from home at the Riverside Church, helping in Mr. Heidt's business office, where Rockefeller money was being poured out as charity to give relief to the desperate poor. Private charity was all the charity there was.

At Riverside, a skyscraper church, I worked on the seventeenth floor of the tower below the carillon of the seventy-two bells. It was an enormous neighborhood Rockefeller Center, with banquet rooms, lecture rooms, card rooms, game rooms, ballroom, nurseries, and a room given over to a collection of toy electric trains for fathers and sons to play with. Postcards were sold in the lobby. The efficient social secretary, Betty House, had charge of a tremendous weekly schedule of events. She invited Margaret Bourke-White up to take photographs for *Life*. Einstein, whose head was carved at the portal among the saints, came one day in December and wandered around the offices like a sad-eyed cherub with a halo of wild gray hair. Anyone might spend his days and nights in a giddy round of uplift and sociability, eating, dancing, praying his life away. Sin was discouraged, of course, but grace was available by appointment months in advance for an interview with Dr. Fosdick, the nearest thing to a confessional the church afforded.

The fact that I was anticlerical didn't bother me, nor would it have worried the three liberal ministers to find a heretic in their midst. ("Not quite a heretic, love," B. said. "You don't know enough of the dogma of any church to deviate from it.") If I was careless of salvation, at least I met them halfway. Once I typed out the Lord's Prayer triple-space for Dr. Carder to read in the pulpit lest he stumble in repeating it.

I didn't go to church on Sunday to hear Dr. Fosdick (six weekdays of piety were enough for me), though I was issued a green ticket to his congregation. A few years before, B. had taken me for a treat to the Fosdick preaching at the Park Avenue Baptist Church. It was hardly a fair test, since I was understandably distracted from the sermon, blinded even, by happening to sit next to Mr. John D. Rockefeller's hat. Beside me on the crimson plush, like a rich communicant except for being upside down, it rested in quiet elegance, a shimmering high hat, its lining aglitter with three initials in pure gold. At the benediction, the owner rose in the pew and, picking up his hat, reached over cordially to shake our hands.

"Good morning," he said. "Glad to see you at the service."

"Good morning, Mr. Rockefeller," said B. "Glad to see you worshiping too."

I used to read Dr. Fosdick's sermons whenever his secretary asked me to track down a quotation, like "Sweets to the sweet" or "Improved means to unimproved ends." He was a quoter, a word man, a man of good faith, a humanist. I might have enjoyed listening to him any day but Sunday.

*

B. continued to work tirelessly at N.Y.U. and the Columbia graduate school, where he entered upon his last year of residence. He was reading in Latin Catullus's love poems to Lesbia and the *Kisses* of Johannes Secundus, which I hated to miss. I had stopped going to school for a while, being badly pressed for time. To read was more urgent than ever, with a new language to learn in the nine-month span —since, too, a book had always represented to me deliverance. My evenings that winter of 1931 were spent in such applied studies as Dr. Morris Slemans' *The Prospective Mother,* Dr. De Lee's *Obstetrics for Nurses,* and Lord Chesterfield's *Letters to His Son,* all of which made instructive sense.

I read Voltaire, and Maeterlinck's *Life of the White Ant.* Yet the real source of inspiration was probably Dr. Johnson—not a man like Thoreau in touch with hoot owls and whippoorwills, but a man who always had something loud and lapidary to say on any subject, even on how to rear a child.

When Boswell asked him, "If, Sir, you were shut up in a castle, and a new-born child with you, what would you do?" Johnson answered sensibly, "Why, Sir, I should not much like my company." But he added, "I would not *coddle* the child."

Another time he declared, "I would put a child into a library (where no unfit books are) and let him read at his choice."

One Sunday in early spring when B. and I were walking in the Bronx Zoo, a woman came up to me at the polar-bear cage. She put both her hands tight across my eyes. "Stay away from the bears, dear," she begged in earnest. "You musn't stare at them like that. You'll mark your unborn child."

I might have said to her, "Madam, this child is already marked. Having been exposed to spectacles like Dr. Johnson, Einstein, and *Lady Chatterley's Lover,* by now he's had it. A few white bears won't do him any harm. Not even a blue-behinded ape."

*

We walked every night twenty blocks or so up and down Broadway in the city we loved, where we fully expected to spend our lives and bring up our children. New York was still the world, though the *World* newspaper was dead, having disappeared on February 27. New York was the navel of the earth, the belly button, where wonders never ceased, where at any moment you might catch sight of yet another marvel: the George Washington Bridge being built with exactitude and symmetry as if by seagulls into a flying span. Or the bearded poet Æ turning up like an Irish prophet, like a golden codger, on the campus one day at Columbia. Or in a theater lobby the back of Gene Tunney's neck.

Saturday nights we went to the theater, to the second balcony, where the dizzying descent at a sharp pitch to one's seat made me realize how far off center my center of gravity had grown to be. We saw God himself and the Angel Gabriel in *The Green Pastures.* At *The Barretts of Wimpole Street,* we watched the rhapsodic love scenes between Robert Browning and Elizabeth Barrett that moved a friend with us, a medieval scholar, to a worried whisper, "What's your guess? Do you believe he'll ever marry her?" We heard Jeritza sing Wagner at the Metropolitan Opera; and it was lovely to walk with the crowds in Times Square afterwards holding fast to a man, then go home with him to read the Sunday *Times* in bed on Saturday night and sleep safe with tomorrow's news of the world already happened.

I must have been in a wonderfully serene state of mind.

83

I had a telephone conversation with Dottie, my bridesmaid, who had recently come to New York to work for *Forbes* magazine. As we talked, two immense fire trucks with all bells clanging drew up in front of my apartment house, the firemen leaped out and raced inside, a crowd quickly gathered. Someone looked up at my window and yelled "Fire!"

I gazed impassively on the noisy scene below. "I think my house is on fire, Dottie," I said into the phone.

She thought I was joking or trying to get rid of her. "It's your condition," she said. "Expectant mothers often imagine they see red flames."

I sniffed. "I seem to smell smoke, too," I said. "Everybody's rushing out of the house now and waving his arms. A woman is hysterical. The janitor is carrying out a dog. The firemen are running their hoses up the front steps."

"Holy God!" cried Dottie. "Are you all right?"

"Yes, I'm sitting beside the fire escape, waiting to be rescued. What were you saying?"

Dottie laughed and hung up. The fire, caused by an explosion in the furnace, was soon extinguished.

*

It all went beautifully till April. Then the excruciating pain returned to B.'s left shin, and the old sickness developed with terrifying rapidity. Soon he was in high fever and delirium. With increased pressure in the bone he became only intermittently conscious, only his tremendous will and vitality kept him alive. At Orthopaedic Hospital, Dr. Farrell operated with two surgeons assisting, and this time so great was the infection that the pus shot to the ceiling. They struggled to save his life.

But he *had* to live. That was the way it had to be. I kept on working, and the nights without him were black with demons and foul fiends. I was terribly afraid. One night after sitting beside his bed, promising over and over I wouldn't have the child till he got home, I left the hospital and walked slowly toward the subway. At Park Avenue I stood waiting for the light to change. The policeman on duty took one horrified look, blew his whistle, held up his hand, and stopped traffic dead in both directions. As I started alone across the wide double-laned avenue in the glare of the headlights, I knew how ridiculous I appeared and tried to laugh. It made me cry bitterly instead.

I used to write him between visits to the hospital. "I think I miss you most when I open the apartment door on these three empty rooms."

And he would manage to scrawl a few words in pencil. "Are you getting enough to eat? Oh, my darling, take care of yourself for me."

New York was a lost city without him, a savage, cruel city in which I had no neighbors. A person across the hall died, someone I had never seen, and the only reason I knew was by the wreath of white carnations on the door.

At three o'clock in the morning my doorbell rang. Fearing some tragic news, I ran to open the door and found a glamorous woman standing there in a fur jacket over a black lace evening gown. She had short waved hair and dangling pearl earrings. She wore perfume, mascara, bright red lipstick.

"I'm your neighbor in the next apartment," she said. "I've forgotten my key. May I use your fire escape?"

She minced across my living room in her high heels. The only flaw in the performance was that she wasn't a woman. She was a man. As he climbed out daintily to the fire escape and stood poised, a gust of wind caught and fluttered his long full skirt. With a little high-pitched scream, clutching at his dress, he disappeared.

*

When B. came back after four weeks in the hospital, on crutches with his leg to the thigh in a heavy plaster cast, he insisted on riding home in the subway. We took a taxi to the uptown subway entrance, where we staggered together down the steps. He said we had to save our money, a dime was the most we could afford to spend.

B. was a stubborn man at times, deaf to reason, unmoved by appeals to common sense. Yet I think he shortly regretted this piece of economy. It was a traumatic way to travel. As the train drew in and we entered the subway car—a haggard, tottering man on crutches beside a balloon-like woman lugging a suitcase and a potted plant—a sigh of pity rose spontaneously from the passengers. Accustomed though they were to pitiful sights during the Depression, here was a picture of pathos verging on the spectacular. Nearly everyone in the car stood up to offer us a seat. Several grasped us by the arm and led us gently down the aisle. I wonder that they didn't take up a collection. We sat from 59th to 116th Street surrounded by their compassion, their deep stares of sympathy and ruth.

I stopped working at Riverside the day of B.'s return. A few days later on May 8 when Dr. Caverly examined me, perhaps for the last time, he inquired casually, "You haven't told me, what kind of baby do you want?"

I was too quick to fall into that trap, to give myself away. "What kind do you think it's going to be?"

He listened to the heartbeat and reflected. "If you were my sister," he said, looking grave, "and I were to make a strictly unprofessional guess, mind you, I would say your baby is a girl."

You have to accept a doctor's decision as informed and final. By her beating heart he knew her sex—what a peculiar way to determine it. B. and I were fools to use the wrong pronoun these many months. This was Ann Bevington, a girl, her turn to be born. She would have to forgo the glory of being male.

Whereupon she became Ann herself, a reality, our little girl. Only once in the next day or two did I slip and say to B., "Shall we have Ann circumcised?" and blushed in shame at being caught hedging my bet.

Sunday, May 10, was a date to sweat out in pure anxiety all day long. The idea of giving birth to a child on Mother's Day seemed the last indignity, a contemptible thing to do. It would be a disgraceful performance, a blight on the infant's life. B. thought it comical, but I had missed by the skin of my teeth being born an April Fool and knew well the danger of such trifling.

*

On May 13, a Wednesday, I woke at 6:00 A.M. with a flickering pain. I reached for my wristwatch and picked up *Northanger Abbey*. The next pain took ten minutes to arrive, a mere gripping and release, brief and unmistakable. When B. awoke, he turned over to smile at me.

"How are you, love?" he said.

"In labor."

"What?" he shouted. He leaped out of bed and hopped around on his good leg, looking for his clothes. "I've got to get you to the hospital!"

"I'm not going till I finish my book," I said.

"What do you mean you're not going? You've *got* to go!"

"I'm going when I finish my book. It's a dozen more pages to the end. She won't be born for hours yet. There's plenty of time."

B. shook his head. "Maybe we should call her Baby Jane Austen," he said.

He took me up in the Whippet about 8:30 that morning and went on to teach three classes at the University. I spent most of the day alone in a pleasant room on Floor O of Sloane Maternity Hospital, reading and eating vanilla ice cream. I started Mrs. Radcliffe's two-volume horror novel *The Mysteries of Udolpho* (the one Jane Austen had parodied) and kept on till midafternoon, when the spasms grew more frequent, rising to new crescendos, falling, climbing to new sharp peaks of pain. When they became violent, I switched to *Charlie Chan Carries On*.

Dr. Caverly was in and out all day, solicitous as if I were his sister. After ten hours of labor, he decided, for fear of injury to the child, upon a Caesarean section.

*

I came drifting back to consciousness engaged in a loud argument. I could hear my insistent voice. "It's a girl," I said to anyone who bent over me. "Ask Dr. Caverly. He knows it's a girl." They had made a mistake; there was some mixup about my baby. Then B. stood beside me on his crutches, and he had tears in his eyes.

"They've balled up the babies," I told him. I ordered him to set them straight. Why did everyone repeat this stupid lie?

"Darling, listen to me," he said laughing. "This baby is a boy."

"How do you know?"

"I've seen him."

"Where?"

"In the nursery."

I closed my eyes. "They're fooling you too," I said.

Even Dr. Caverly played out the little comedy. "An eight-pound boy, ma'am," he told me lightly. "Isn't that what you said you wanted?"

I lay in a half-stupor, struggling to think it over. Why the cruel deception? Was I too ill to be told? After a while I roused enough to ask the nurse to bring the baby to me. She went to the nursery and soon returned, laying the child beside me on the pillow. I turned my head. A string of blue beads around its neck spelled out the name, "Baby Bevington"—obviously they refused to admit what its sex was. I stared intensely at the clear blue eyes, the tiny red mouth, the even features so like B.'s, the well-shaped blond head.

"I was right," I said. "It's a girl."

Calmly the nurse unwrapped the blanket from the child and took off its garments. She picked it up and held it naked before my eyes, giving the occasion its due.

"There's your girl. Isn't she pretty?" she said.

I was stunned, beside myself with surprise and rapture. It was the real article. It was beautiful. It was David.

Grant him born, then.

6

When David was eight weeks old in July, we took him to the Flanderses' farm. He rode between us in the Whippet, lying in a well-padded melon crate, up to the Berkshire hills near Pittsfield, Massachusetts. At the bottom of the perpendicular hill leading to the farmhouse, the exhausted car gasped and stalled. I got out and climbed the steep road on foot, hauling David up like a box of melons, while B. coaxed the tired little Whippet to try again. Our child would know early what a hill was.

This was the beginning of life with the Flanders family through twelve magic summers. When I think of the play *You Can't Take It with You* about Grandpa Vanderhof's crazy houseful, I think of us at the farm—both because everybody who came was free to move in and enjoy himself, and because it was true, we couldn't take it with us after all. It was a time of immense pleasure among life-loving, life-enhancing people, and then it was over. None of us could have guessed in those days the horror that lay ahead.

B. and I had met the Flanderses during the winter. Donald Flanders (known since college as Moll, like Defoe's Moll) was an assistant professor of mathematics at New York University, a man of whom B. said after having lunch with him at the Faculty Club, "I've just met one of the saints. I want him for my friend."

When Sally and Moll invited us to their Morningside Avenue apartment for coffee one evening, I went eagerly to meet them. I was sorry and then incensed that I had gone.

They lived in a ramshackle building in a tawdry neighborhood, and their railroad flat was in a state of disarray that looked cyclonic. It was not clutter, it was chaos. Though tidy myself, I knew that people weren't more lovable for being neat, or for being sloppy either. You couldn't use that thin a yardstick.

Sally motioned us to overstuffed chairs occupied by two small children, a cat, and a dog. "Get down, Spinach," she said to the dog. She was extremely pregnant with her third child, a stocky woman in her thirties with a mannish bob of straight, light-brown hair, a round face, and no makeup. She was a chain-smoker with a frog in her throat. Since the staring children and animals didn't stir, we removed the debris from two straight chairs and sat down.

Sally sat opposite on the piano stool, and Moll rushed in belatedly to shake our hand. If he was a saint, it was a distracted one. Clearly he failed to recognize us or recall why we had come. He sat bemused, wrapped in deep thought, scratching his hair where it had receded from his forehead, crossing and recrossing his legs—a tallish, dark, thin man of great intensity of concentration. A knotty problem in his head was in the process of being solved. While he tussled with it, we waited in silence.

91

Sally said briskly, "Good! With four voices we can get to work on some Palestrina. You'll have to sing soprano, whatever your range," pointing a finger at me. "Alto is as high as I go."

"I don't sing," I said flatly.

That broke Moll's trance. He and Sally looked as astonished as if I had said I couldn't read or write.

"I'll help you if you want help," Moll said. "We sing for the love of it, nothing professional. Don't worry about a polished performance. Just read through a part."

"You can do a solfège," Sally said. "Never mind the Latin words."

"I can't read through a part," I said mulishly. "I'm tone-deaf. I don't sing."

With a sigh as if to say Why in hell did she come? Sally stood up and leafed through the piles of music on top of the piano. She extracted three copies of the *Musica Sacra* and handed two around to B. and Moll.

"If she won't try, we'll simply have to sing without her," she said. "All right, everybody, start with the three-part Lotti, page 47, *'Vere languores nostros.'* I'll take the first tenor, Bev the second tenor, Moll the bass. Oh, what *fun!*"

I went indignant to the far corner of the room, picked up a book, and fuming with rage read all evening. Nobody spoke to me. They tuned and disported themselves, sometimes doubled up with laughter. At midnight Sally served the coffee, still treating me like a mannerless child, and we could go home. They had sung for three solid hours.

When next I saw Sally, in February, she had given birth to Jane. B. asked me to visit her in the hospital, and exploding in anger I refused. Then he *told* me to go, which I resented more loudly. His friendship with Moll meant a great deal to him. He said I could stop being stiff-necked and learn to put up with Sally.

"It seems to me a lowdown, heartless thing to ask," I cried in fury.

"That is because, dearest, you are a dunce," he said.

"I am not a dunce!"

"I know," he said. "I was only quoting."

"For the love of God, B.! Will you stop *quoting* every minute?" I yelled.

"Peace, good pintpot."

Sally lay smoking Fatimas in her hospital bed, arms akimbo, full of bounce. Having a baby was no ordeal for her. While I sat coldly silent, outraged to be there, she talked for an hour about herself, how she had gone to Vassar with Edna St. Vincent Millay; how she had gone abroad with John Dos Passos, or at least on the same boat; how she had met a saint from Haverford and married him, borne him three perfect children, and had a perfect life. She had perfect relatives and perfect friends. She told me she assumed that people should please her, not that she should try to please them. God, I thought, how boring.

"That's because I'm a Murray," she said.

I didn't ask the meaning of this remark. I couldn't have cared less. Later I learned, not from Sally (who had no snobbery in her, only a vast contentment with her lot) that it meant she was one of the Murrays of Murray Hill. She was a birthright Quaker too, who had resigned from the Meeting but still used the plain language. She said *thee* to those she loved, to her family and the people who pleased her.

"Thee is expecting a child," she said abruptly as I rose to go.

"Yes."

"When?"

"In May."

"I'll come to see thee then. I know thee hates like hell to admit it, but I think we're going to be friends."

93

I took the warm hand she offered me. She had extraordinary gray eyes, capable of much compassion. There was approval in her voice and lovingkindness. Strangely enough I realized what a good friend she could be. She *liked* me. In spite of myself I liked her.

*

The farmhouse stood at the end of a long driveway, in a wild ragged setting of woods and partial clearing. It belonged there, like the elderberry bushes, the deer and woodchucks, the hemlocks, the white birches—an old house of unpainted, weathered gray clapboard, stark and boxlike with a high roof and no porch. A large sagging barn loomed up behind.

The place always gave me the creeps. It looked lonely, even haunted, filled to the rafters though it was with noisy laughing children and equally noisy grownups. It seemed lost and adrift up in the hills, not a summer place but a remote hill farm, banished and forgotten, out of touch with the world and out of caring. You would expect the people who lived there to be half-savage and illiterate. There was something chilling about it that made me want to weep—a loneliness, an untamed look, a desolation, a solitude. Perhaps that was why, in its unlikelihood, I came to love it so deeply.

It had a grim history of murder. Frank McCabe used to tell the story, Frank who with his brother Pete still farmed a few acres a mile away over the next hill. It went back to the time when George Crew, who owned the place, married one of the Green girls of Green Hollow, Mary by name, and brought her to live on this lonely farm. Her sister Pearl came along too, an oldmaid schoolteacher, who hated George with a passion.

She tried several times to kill him, the story went. Once as George passed through the kitchen, he found the outside door standing open and behind it the tips of a pair of rubber boots just showing below the edge of the door. Flinging it shut, he discovered Pearl hiding there, dressed unaccountably in hip boots with an upraised axe in her hands. Not long after, George was found dead in the barn, lying in a pool of blood. According to the family, he had been repairing the floor boards and a board had snapped up, hitting a horse standing in its stall. The horse had reared and kicked him to death.

"It was a funny thing," Frank McCabe used to say. "They claimed that pony rared up and kicked George with its shoe and brained him. Maybe it did," shaking his head. "But me and Pete, we come over and seen enough to satisfy us. That pony wasn't even shod."

On the night before the funeral, Pearl slipped out in the dark, set fire to the barn, and when it blazed high ran off into the woods to hide. The flaming barn burned to the ground. The way Frank McCabe figured, Pearl was only getting rid of the bloody monkeywrench before it was found and used against her.

Pearl died years later in the state lunatic asylum. The last of the Greens still alive in the countryside was her sister Susie, married to halfwitted Lester Bolton, living in a shack somewhere in these thickly wooded hills. On moonlight nights Susie, mad as the vex'd sea, howled like a hound dog and bayed at the moon. We often heard her barking as we walked along the moonlit road or sat out under the stars. "My God, there's Susie!" we would say in hushed voices, shuddering at the eerie sound. I'd rather listen to a spook any time than to mad Susie baying her heart out under a bright moon.

Moll and Sally bought the old Crew place, standing empty and lost, abandoned for years. They chased out the bats, kept the mice and chipmunks, added a few improvements like a drilled well, an upright piano, some peonies

and lilac bushes, and named it Skipton—which hardly suited
its nature but Sally named everything.

Sally's sister Bobby and her husband Tom Fansler had
found a second farm, also unoccupied, on the opposite
hillside and bought it. They named it Heyshott, a white
frame farmhouse with unpainted barns, neglected orchards
and pasturelands. You could holler across the valley from
Skipton to Heyshott, but it took ten minutes to walk around
by the dirt road, down one steep hill and toiling up the
next.

The two farms and their families made a company that
in good time I loved more than any other I have known.
They became my family, closer than blood kin, the friends
of a lifetime. But for a day or two I had to fight it out
with Sally.

*

Sally was a boss, running the show singlehanded, bawling
out orders like a camp director, ruling her empire like
Catherine of Russia. From the moment of our arrival that
afternoon she told me what to do, when to do it, and how
to bring up my child.

"Go change Dave's pants and put him to bed, *quickly*,"
she said before we reached the front door. "Come back and
tea will be ready. After tea, we'll sing."

"It's time for his orange juice," I said.

"It is *not* time for orange juice. Don't be an idiot. It's
time for tea," Sally said. "Put him in the back bedroom
where we can't hear him if he cries. And don't keep us
waiting. Hurry up!"

Infuriated, I went to do as she said. My feeling for days
after was one of open hostility. "I'm damned if I will!" I
thought each time she pushed me around. "I'll do as I
damn please!" Yet when she told me not to wear lipstick

in the country or to take my nose out of a book, I muttered to myself and, sorely insulted, obeyed. She was
undermining my character. At least I was allowed to walk
barefoot in the grass.

B. caught on, but not I. He relaxed from the start, let
her manage him, ignored my suffering, and enjoyed himself. Though in general B. hated bossy women as man-eaters
and emasculators, he recognized at once the essential difference in Sally. He grasped what it took me years to accept—which was the infinite wisdom, the profit to oneself,
of giving Sally her way. If you yielded and let her, she
would run your life as a personal service better than you
could yourself. She had a natural bent for it. She gave her
time and her heart, planning your duties and multiplying
your pleasures, directing your existence. It took not so much
a submissive mind as a generous one to grasp her worth.
She offered her great talent for living, her love of life. And
it was all free.

Accepting Sally on her own terms was a bitter lesson,
hard but reasonable. It worked to my endless advantage
and enriched my life. Harder still, now that she is dead,
is to write of her at all when it was she, the bountiful one,
who was so passionately alive.

*

After breakfast next morning, Sally sent the men to the
cellar to work ankle-deep in mud at jacking up the foundations of the house. Upstairs resembled a medieval
kitchen, with me the scullion set to preparing the day's
food—cutting up string beans, shelling peas, peeling po-
tatoes—while Sally made blackberry jam, canned tomatoes
in the pressure cooker, and washed diapers in the kitchen
sink. Peter, five, and Ellen, four, ran whooping in and out
of the house. The two babies, each in a cardboard carton

at my feet, alternately slept or screamed. Sally took this idle leisure time, free of distraction, to teach me how to sing.

I objected strenuously, clenching my teeth, cursing her under my breath, but it did no good. She began with school rounds and progressed to simple canons.

Man's life's a vapor [we sang]
Full of woes.
He cuts a caper,
Down he goes.
Down, down, down, down, down he goes.

Sally's voice was husky, the notes came out a little blurred but accurate enough. *"Non nobis, Domine, non nobis,"* she rumbled, a cigarette dangling from her mouth. "Go ahead! *Sing!* Thee comes in two beats behind me." She drilled like an army sergeant, beating out the time with a soapy hand from the kitchen sink. Meanwhile the pressure cooker gathered steam and threatened to explode. The babies woke and wailed, with scarcely a hope of being heard or attended to.

Moll called out from the cellar, "Sounds pretty good from here. Her voice is true, it reminds me of my mother's."

"She's been lying all the while, damn her," answered Sally. "We'll do some four-part Palestrina after tea."

It was the Palestrina Mass in perpetual canon that became the master work to bind us together in a four-part eternal friendship. Moll drilled us that summer as if we were the Mormon Tabernacle Choir, and we laughed and wept to hear ourselves, especially the first time we managed to keep going from the splendid opening, the *Kyrie eleison,* through the *Gloria in excelsis Deo* to the powerful, tremendous Amen of the *Credo.* I had never known the pride of polyphonic song before, but I knew it now. We sat huddled on the lawn on a blanket, with Moll up on his knees to lead us—Moll, who heard every note and provided one when we lost it, who carried us struggling mightily through the lofty *Sanctus,* the shouting *Hosanna in excelsis,* the prayerful *Benedictus,* the melodious, seraphic *Agnus dei,* after which Sally embraced her child prodigy, and we four fell back exhausted on the blanket, helpless with laughter at our sweating but victorious performance, the holy conquest of Palestrina.

And of the four of us choristers who achieved this triumph, I am the only one left, the only one still alive to say that it was so. And I say that it was so.

*

Tom Fansler taught English at New York University. Bobby, his wife, was a lecturer at the Metropolitan Museum of Art, a woman of infinite charm who collected friends like art works, and the friends adorned her life and turned up uninvited at either house, sure of a welcome—artists who hurriedly set up an easel to paint the View, art critics and historians who sat down to discuss it. Musicians gathered over the weekends, fiddler and cellist to play chamber music with Moll. At sunset children walked the road up to Pop Gowan's for the milk. We danced on the lawn to Moll's fiddle or played a fierce game of bowls that kept on after dark to flashlights and lanterns. Most of all we talked, dogged talkers who never flagged nor failed. And while we talked we laughed.

B. and I climbed daily the hill to the little Bacon Hill schoolhouse with the idea of buying it and staying on forever in this countryside. It was an abandoned one-room schoolhouse equipped with scarred desks, a potbellied stove, two outdoor toilets, and a yardful of sugar maples. The two toilets made it somehow irresistible.

Once when Moll and I were returning from Canaan, the

small village two miles away where we bought groceries, he drove me up past mad Susie's shack in the hills. At the sound of the car, Susie rushed out of the house brandishing a large butcher knife, her stringy gray hair hanging down her back, her eyes crazy and glittering. She raced to the road waving her arms, yelling obscenities as she came, and when Moll politely drew up she thrust her head inside the front window where I sat holding David on my lap. Pointing her knife at my throat, she grinned like a witch, staring into my eyes.

"Lift up your skirts, dear, and let him put it to you," she cried, menacing with her knife. "It's all men want anyhow."

"Listen to her," said Moll. "Do you hear the natural music, the simple, easy rhythm, the flow of her speech? It's almost a folk song."

"She sounds like a poet," I said dryly.

*

I don't know how much less extraordinary the summer might have been had I grown up with a big family or been part of a tumult before. Since B. was one of five children, it appeared less remarkable to him. But I was shaken and happy in this roaring household.

For however violent or calm the intervals, it was good, it was lovely at the Farm. It was as if—the Kantian as if—all would be well and we would stay absurdly young and alive forever. Much virtue in *as if*. Our only fault was that, however ardent of life, we were unable to do so.

7

"Life is just a bowl of cherries" went a popular song in 1931. The banks began to collapse that fall—the great Bank of the United States had failed—and by the end of the year there were some ten million (soon to be fifteen million) unemployed. People lived in tents and caves, slept in doorways, flophouses, boxcars, telephone booths. They scoured the dumps for food, and they starved. There were hunger marches, coal strikes, lockouts, suicides. It was an ailing world, a sickening time of chronic misery and despairing lives. Some of the losers were our friends.

In October B. and I moved to an apartment in the Bronx, exchanging one campus for another, Columbia for New York University, and I became no longer a graduate student but a faculty wife wheeling a baby carriage. By now I couldn't have found a job. I was one of the unemployed.

We lived in a grimy, nondescript apartment house on Loring Place, our windows looking out on a narrow court, where the occupants of the building save ourselves were Irish Catholics, inclined to be combative and rowdy—lace-curtain Irish, who took out their fighting with their wives. Their church was St. Nicholas Tolentine on Fordham Road, which sold lottery tickets and raffled off a Ford car from time to time, and after it was invented had weekly Bingo like a common gambling joint. When a neighbor's child asked B. down in the court one day if our little boy would soon go to confession, he roared, "No! We're Mohammedans."

I had a whirldry washing machine from Macy's—a table model that held eight diapers—and a few books by which to rear David. Neither worked. The machine danced about and toppled off the kitchen sink because I overloaded it. The books disheartened me. Written by spinsters at Teachers College, experts on home guidance, they stressed toilet training one month after birth and no pampering of the child or lavishing of love.

"Baby care is a great art," said the bulletin *Infant Care* issued by the U.S. Department of Labor in its 1930's phase. You must build your baby's character by regularity of meals, sleep, and elimination. Teach him regularity. Give him a smile of approval for regularity. Never pick him up between meals.

Yet the rigid schedule of feedings (6:00, 10:00, 2:00, 6:00, 10:00), supplemented by doses around the clock of orange juice, prune juice, tomato juice, cod liver oil, and if all else failed boiled water, meant that David was seldom in bed, what with being put on the pot (once an hour, the book said), weighed, bathed, oiled, dressed, undressed, changed, aired, exercised, and taken to the doctor for shots. Any time left over was devoted to the sterilizing of bottles and toys. I was never so antiseptic. There had appeared yet no Dr. Spock to simplify life, no diaper service, no rubber pants, no strained vegetables or apple sauce. There was only Conditioning.

John B. Watson, founder of Behaviorism, left me with a permanent scar, stabbed with remorse and a sense of inadequate parenthood, especially after I heard him speak one morning at a session for mothers at Macy's. During the question period, women stood humbly to confess their failure—how they had picked up their child in infancy when he cried and he had turned into a juvenile delinquent. Dr. Watson wearily shook his head, repeating the elementary lesson. "Never hug or kiss your baby," he said. "Never let him sit in your lap." I gave no testimony, though David was doubtless ruined by love already, conditioned to the stimuli in his environment. It was too late in life to recondition him.

At five months he barely managed to pass the intelligence tests at the six-month level as formulated by Dr. Arnold Gesell in *The Mental Growth of the Pre-School Child*—that is, he banged a spoon well, put his bottle nipple first in his mouth, and splashed in the tub. But he probably had a mother fixation or an Oedipus complex for life.

I held him in my lap anyway, recklessly fondling him, and it seemed to me love did him no outward harm. He was not one to fuss or cry. We spent our lives together for better or worse, most of it outdoors. During the morning in the sunlit court, the street musicians sang "Mother Machree" or a hurdygurdy stopped in to play "Santa Lucia." After lunch I sat on a park bench beside his carriage and read aloud to him the book I was reading—the *History of the Novel in England* or the letters of Abelard and Heloise. On March 1 while he safely slept I read to myself the terrifying details of the kidnaping of the Lindbergh baby. His diet printed

in the newspaper was the same as David's. Then my friend
Lois Knowles had a baby and joined me on the dusty bench
—the Madonnas of Fordham Road.

*

The faculty wives, sisters, cousins, and aunts met once a
month in the downstairs parlor of the Men's Faculty Club.
Calling ourselves the Faculty Women's Club, we wore hats
and gloves, sat in prim rows on folding chairs, and listened
to Madam President flutteringly introduce the Program
Chairman, who flutteringly introduced the Speaker of the
afternoon, exactly like the cartoons of Helen E. Hokinson.
The Speaker would be a squeak-voiced, elderly professor
badgered into giving us a free talk on Paraguay or the
League of Nations. Once the Chancellor himself, Elmer
Ellsworth Brown, came to praise us in our role to a grateful
University of loyal wives, mothers, aunts, and whatnot. We
were the inspiration and the lyre, he said (spelling it out:
l-y-r-e); we were the muse and the harp.

I went regularly to the meetings because B. came home
to give me the Monday afternoon off. But I didn't like going. I disliked being a faculty wife. It was a great disappointment, frustrating and dull, an emptyheaded role. Afterwards I mimicked the ladies to make B. laugh—the cocked
little finger over the teacup, the glazed look during the
lecture, the simpering applause, the genteel murmurs, the
secretary's pronunciation of *mesdames* as if it were mess
dames. But it was no good. It was cheap humor, besides
which I had no call to condescend, being properly one of
them, no wiser, no better dressed, no better informed on
Paraguay.

Lord Melbourne once explained to the young Queen
Victoria: "It's very rare that women are kind to one
another." He might have added, women in an organized
group. Women are snubbers. I found them cold and formal,

not inclined to make friends. At our teas to which the faculty was invited, we appointed a number of "floaters," whose official duty it was to be gracious, to move among the guests and see they weren't actually rebuffed or ignored. When old Professor Herring and his two daughters attended one of these functions, a faculty wife ushered them in. "I just floated in three herrings," she said.

Madam President tried to heighten the tone of the Faculty Women's Club by setting up a few study groups for the self-improving members who agreed to speak French, play bridge, or read a book together. The one I got into, by timidly raising my hand at a meeting, called itself The Scribblers. It was started by Ethel Harris, wife of a professor of engineering, who had sold thirteen short stories to the *Saturday Evening Post.* This looked like fast company, yet we four who signed up with Ethel were dabblers and dreamers. We were wives seeking an outlet, a way to occupy our nonexistent leisure and entertain our minds.

We met one night a month at somebody's house, and we became five devoted friends by avoiding criticism and pouring out only undiminished praise. We exchanged applause. Ethel Harris was a witty person, who wrote her extremely long short stories on the backs of giltedged securities that had proved worthless since the market crash. She claimed to have enough bad stocks in her possession to outlast her writing career. Ethel was an eccentric, the kind who would pick up a frozen sparrow (as she did one snowy morning on Fifth Avenue), thrust it into her bosom, and go shopping at Lord and Taylor's. There before the startled customers she began to chirp and twitter as the bird thawed out.

"Did madam say something?" asked the clerk.

For answer she gave a loud squawk, her breast fluttered, and out flew the bird to sail overhead around the store. I liked her very much.

Grace Musser's husband was dean of the graduate school,

Grace Gove's was an English instructor, and I think Julia Nock's husband taught history. As faculty wives we were distinguished by our spouse's rank and the subject he taught. Some wives believed in strict protocol and the humbling of instructors.

The reading on club night of Ethel's latest novelette, full of romantic love scenes set in Venice and spy plots in the Balkans, followed steadily by Grace Musser's, Grace Gove's, and Julia Nock's, more than exhausted the evening. It exhausted us, spending our passions, using up our supply of compliments. Fiction took us to midnight, after which came my belated turn, like one rising to sing "God Bless America" or speak the benediction. My few and hastily recited stanzas brought to a close the literary part of the program. It was time, thank God, for the refreshments.

At least I had an excuse for writing a verse a month to keep up my membership with The Scribblers. I wrote for love not gain, in the amateur spirit, finding no reason to take myself to heart. It gave me a wild night out with my friends. A night with a cultural air.

*

For other nights out, B. and I hired Mrs. Penfold, the campus babysitter, who minded the baby at twenty-five cents an hour. We booked her sometimes a month in advance, spending to my horror as much as one hundred dollars a year for four hundred hours on the town.

Four hundred hours? Where on earth did we go? We went to the movies separately to save money, paying the price of loneliness. I rushed out of *Wuthering Heights* one night blinded by tears to stumble home alone. When B. saw a movie, he forgot its name, and if in exasperation I asked who was in it he said "Beatrice Lillie." Since the days of Gilda Gray, the shimmy dancer, and Mae Murray of the beestung lips, he hadn't looked twice at movie queens. He liked Maurice Chevalier after somebody told him he was the spitting image of Chevalier. Actually he was. They had the same smile, the same eye for a pretty woman.

On Saturday night we danced at the Faculty Club, brightly lit and sedate as a church social. It was lit, not we. When Ned Knowles told me during a waltz I had the prettiest legs in the Bronx, prettier than Jankin's, the fifth husband of the Wife of Bath, I knew he spoke in utter sobriety. A drinking man would have included the other four boroughs. But then we were usually sober, even during these wide-open days of Prohibition—so wide-open that men made a living by stopping a prospect on the street and with a wink showing him a pint whiskey bottle in the breast pocket. "Wanna buy some cold tea?" he would whisper. And the man would buy it and take home a bottle of cold tea.

We had no money to spend for liquor, being accustomed at our parties to serving hot cocoa with homemade cookies, or Ovaltine for a nightcap. Twice B. made a batch of homebrew in the kitchen washtubs, smelling up the apartment like a brewery. Now and then a diaper fell into it, though I don't believe that accounted for the terrible taste. "A bit yeasty," B. would say. It was better than making gin in the bathtub, but not much better.

The cocktail party was something else, even if few of us could afford on our salaries to give one. We went when an invitation came our way to these marathon affairs, routine in the Village, fifty people crammed breast to breast in a smokefilled room from 5:00 P.M. to midnight—fifty turbulent people, stayed with flagons of bootleg liquor, sober as Rabelais (who said he drank no more than a sponge). It seemed a graceless way to love your neighbor. How could you love yourself in that din and racket, to the whiskey tempo and the gin fling?

After midnight those of us still conscious and on our feet, our sails in the wind, pot-valiant, went bowling at an allnight bowling alley, where someone reeling off-balance always forgot to let go of his ball and followed it on his face in a headlong lunge down the alley. In the middle of the night we attended the six-day bicycle race at Madison Square Garden, to watch the riders steer around the track in a hypnotic trance, waiting for one of them to take advantage of the general stupor and steal a lap.

On our return by subway just before dawn, twelve hours later and owing her three dollars, Mrs. Penfold would be sitting brighteyed under the lamp, a tiny grayhaired woman working a crossword puzzle, unreproachful and serene.

"Good evening, Mrs. Pinfeather," B. addressed her, unaware of his slip. "May I see you home?" He whirled off with her through the Bronx and once as they sped along reached down and turned off the headlights, convinced for some reason that the car was on fire. The old lady rode in pitch darkness busily chatting as if the sun still shone. Nor did she refuse to sit for us again.

"I always feel safe with Mr. Bevington," she said on her return. "The Lord is my shepherd."

*

But the times grew rapidly worse, the crisis deepened. Calamity stalked us nearer home. The suicides were happening on our own street. On a night when B. and I walked to the corner for a package of cigarettes, we came within inches of being hit by the hurtling body of a man who had thrown himself from the roof of the apartment house next door. He fell crashing to the sidewalk, a stranger of perhaps fifty, and we saw him die. This was the second time such a thing had happened to B.—twice a man had plummeted out of the sky to death at his feet. Yet the crowd gathering that night wasn't large or much excited. No one asked, "Was it an accident?" A few murmured their curiosity: "Who was he?"

"Was he out of work?" Then the police came and quietly asked us to move on.

I remember reading Montaigne that year, who thought the way to live life was on its own terms. Some of his words on the subject shocked and dismayed me. He said for him the crown of happiness was the remembrance of other men's misfortunes: "I am always picturing, under a thousand forms, the lives of those whom fortune or their own mistakes have tossed and submerged." Thus he sought to steady himself. I tried to grasp his view, even to allow its wisdom—the idea that none escape, suffering is common to all—but it seemed callous. There were too many tragic misfortunes for one to take comfort in sharing the human lot.

The lowest ebb of the Depression was the terrible fall and winter of 1932, the fourth winter of it. This was the blackest year, when we reached rock bottom and were worse off even than we knew. It read, more than one observed, like the Book of Job. The song hit now was savage and realistic, "Brother, Can You Spare a Dime?" for the dispossessed, the scavengers, the squatters camped along the Hudson and in Central Park, living in tarpaper shacks and packing boxes. None of them could spare a wooden nickel. Hoovervilles, these living quarters were called. And Herbert Hoover was still our deluded President.

He had promised to banish poverty, keep us on the gold standard, with a vanishing poorhouse, a chicken-in-every-pot, two-cars-in-every-garage. It sounded silly when he said it. Applied to starvation it was unforgivable. "I have no fears for the future of our country," he announced in 1929. Too soon the country, "bright with hope," staggered with the turn of the wheel, the wreckage of lives, the outcasts, the homeless. A third of the nation was in misery. And he was still President.

I nearly voted for Franklin D. Roosevelt in the fall of

1932 because in a campaign speech he said, "Judge me by the enemies I have made." Roosevelt was feared and hated, surely as much as Hoover but by a different class of people— the rich, not the starving. Yet unlike B. I stayed loyal to the Socialists, hoping, I guess, that Norman Thomas would step forward and create a new society to take the place of a dying capitalism. Whatever my hopes, I voted innocently and blindly in dissent.

It was not only America beset. England had its ruinous Depression and the dole. Germany's Depression had brought Hitler to power. In January Hitler became Chancellor, and already there were protest meetings in New York because of Nazi atrocities against Jews. Soon the Jews themselves began to arrive from Germany in a steady stream.

*

All the while, in a worsening world, B. and I were happy— not through the misfortunes of others but through our own fortune. We were not exactly alone. Others were yet un-licked—like Father Divine up in Harlem, who had established himself as Almighty God in a nonsegregated Heaven, crying joyfully, "Peace, it's truly wonderful!" B. and I believed in our luck, confident of a saner world than this. It might have to come through bloody revolution, but it would come. Our children would be the gainers. They would prosper in the end.

Early in September I telephoned Dr. Caverly at his office.

"Tell me, please, when are you planning to take your summer vacation?" I asked.

"I've already had it."

"I mean next summer—1933."

"*Next* summer? Hmmm, well, I don't know. Hadn't given it a thought. Why?"

"I was thinking of having another child."

He laughed. "Here we go again," he said.

"At your convenience," I said.

"Not at all. At your convenience, madam, and your pleasure," he said. "Always at your service. How about letting me off for the Fourth of July?"

"Done," I said.

David was a little towhead, running about like a small beagle dog with his tail in the air, able to carry a tune. Every afternoon he went to the hall closet and yammered for the portable victrola to be brought out, then stood beside it and gravely listened to the whole of Haydn's "Surprise Symphony." Though he knew nine songs by heart, including "Danny Boy" and "Where Has the Bow-Wow Gone?" he greatly preferred Haydn. Each night in bed he sang himself to sleep with the stately measures of the second movement of the "Surprise"—*"Da-da, da-da, da-da, da,"* or varied the rhythm as Haydn did, *"Da-da-da, da-da-da, da-da-da, da."* At a year and a half, he was all but ready to sing the Palestrina Mass with the Flanderses. I thought to myself, "The returns are coming in."

My grandmother Smith died during that year and left among her effects an old radio, which was handed down to me since no one else in the family wanted it. They all had radios. B. and I had bought one for my mother to assuage her loneliness, but we objected to such a gadget in the house. We wanted the *Encyclopaedia Britannica* instead. My grandmother's radio console proved a tawdry object, large and offensive with its Gothic false-front of mahogany veneer arched like a cathedral door, blaring forth Amos 'n' Andy, Lum 'n' Abner, Popeye, the crooners, the quizzers, the Town Crier—"This is Woollcott speaking"—handsomely sponsored by Cream of Wheat.

On March 4 Roosevelt's warm, confident voice came over everybody's radio, telling us to banish fear, "nameless, unreasoning, unjustified terror." Every bank in the country had locked its doors, in New York State only that morning, some never to reopen. The whole system had collapsed like a tottering wall, the almighty dollar had disappeared. Were we supposed to live now without *money?* This time my mother was one of the victims, having lost by this catastrophe every penny of her savings that she hadn't lost earlier in worthless stocks. Her salary from the Erie had been pared down to starvation wages, and she was obliged to take off three relief days a month without pay. She had her backbone left, her courage, that was about all.

When I snatched up David and hurried to Hornell to try to comfort my mother, she was living without meat or much fuel, looking for a cheaper house to rent though she paid only fifteen dollars a month where she was.

The letters B. and I wrote each other during this brief separation were, as usual, love letters, anything but newsy, given up to desolate protestation and avowal of love. We clamored the moment we were parted, and no trivia like world events got mentioned. When I had to leave him, I learned only that he was losing his mind without me and replied with the same passionate complaint. The world was well lost.

But this time I wrote to him: "When will the revolution and the shooting begin?" And he answered in the darkest possible words: "Oh, my love, these are frightful days to be alive. There seems now a likelihood of a general European war, which means another world war. After that, what next? The end of the planet?" Without these words, I might have forgotten how threatening the hour was, how the doom was upon us. I wouldn't have believed we were aware of, already waiting for, the coming of World War II.

*

The baby we waited for (more confidently) was due the end of July. In June the three of us moved into Professor Jones's house for the summer. Professor Jones, a scholarly bachelor who lived with his mother a few blocks away on West 179th Street, had given us his house rentfree while they spent the summer in Massachusetts. It was a big house, filled with life-sized portraits of his grim New England ancestors, and it came as a godsend. B. had been hired to teach the immense freshman English course in the summer school at New York University, after figuring to the penny that his salary would equal the cost of having another baby.

"This one is on me," he said graciously.

To match his gesture, I decided to make my first maternity dress. On a scorching day in June I went shopping at Macy's, where after long choosing I bought a sensible matronly print to cover my matronly figure. Three dollars for a dress was an extravagance, but I had to wear something.

I loved shopping at Macy's because of the mirror. A full-length looking glass (one in particular) stood next to the escalator on the second floor, before which I always stopped for inspection and inventory. During the past six years in New York, I had peered into it at infrequent intervals—not that my face pleased me ("I have seen better faces in my time" *King Lear*) or, by this date, my figure either—not in vanity but in hope. It provided a way to stay in touch with the self-regarding self, measure time and tide, keep track of one's likeness in the midst of buffeting fortune. "Live and die before a mirror," said Baudelaire. "No vanity's displayed," said Yeats,

> *I'm looking for the face I had*
> *Before the world was made.*

It was in a sense a study of survival.

Some women, of course, prefer to give up staring into

mirrors. Amy Lowell shrouded hers in towels to avoid a glimpse of her person. Lady Mary Wortley Montagu felt too mortified to look again after reaching her middle fifties. La Castiglione, the prettiest woman in Europe, had every mirror smashed. It must have been loss of beauty that bothered them, not loss of character.

The mirror at Macy's served the public gaze, a timepiece, an hourglass to say how late the hour was. In an impersonal manner it had faithfully reflected me in many guises of loneliness and content, sometimes wispy or wan, distraught, once in tears, once on the day of my marriage the way I wanted to be—radiantly happy. It had given me a kaleidoscopic face, a versatile one. Like Heraclitus I was led to speculation that all is flux: one cannot step into the same stream or look into the same mirror twice.

On this morning I stopped once more for advice as to what the image revealed: a noticeably pearshaped female resembling a suburban housewife, short of stature and breath, wearing a mild expression with no visible signs of discontent. I smiled tolerantly at her, yet something was awry. She looked pitiful, tired and hot (it was a sweltering day) and unnaturally pale. Sweat stood in beads on her forehead. To my startled eyes she began to droop and sag, swaying drunken. Her knees buckled. She staggered before the now oddly weaving, distorting mirror, a wilderness of mirrors. . .

I turned and ran to the down escalator, trying desperately to reach the outside door in time, to breathe the reviving air. The last thing I remember was stepping out into the dense noonday crowd on Thirty-fourth Street.

"She's going to have a *baby!*" a woman's voice announced shrilly, and a man's, "Call an ambulance, somebody!" I opened my eyes. I was lying flat on the sidewalk, encircled by a hundred staring city faces. Blurred and solemn, they pressed close around me, hemming me in. Was I naked? I felt a panic in my throat, a sudden terror, a frantic need to scream.

I struggled to sit up. A woman leaned over to pat my face. "There, there, here's your package, lie still," she said, buzzing like a blowfly. "They'll take you to the hospital in a minute. Are you hungry?" When people collapsed on the street these days it was usually from hunger.

A policeman worked his way through the crowd, parting it with both arms. "Break it up, break it up," he said. "On your way. Give her air."

He looked down at me at his feet. "It was the mirror. I looked in Macy's mirror," I told him incoherently. "I want to go home. I want a taxi, *please.*"

He helped me to my feet, brushed me off, and summoning a taxi lifted me gently into it. The cab driver groaned to collect such a battered passenger. "What'll I do with her?" he asked, but the policeman motioned him to move on. The crowd had already slipped back into its pattern, rushing to and fro on the sidewalk.

I thought of Maria Theresa, to whom the great panoramic dramas of her life always happened when she was pregnant. And she had sixteen children.

＊

Dr. Caverly set the date of the baby's birth by Caesarean section for July 31. Again he freely predicted a girl. This time I laughed, agreeing it was no doubt so, a better than even chance. He couldn't afford to be wrong twice. Ann Bevington was ready to make her belated appearance on earth, with the unmistakable heartbeat of a girl. Let it anyway be a robust heart.

On the night of July 30, B. took me to Sloane Hospital in the Whippet as before, then returned to David. The two of them slept on a blanket on the handkerchief lawn behind the Jones house. It was an unbearably hot, breathless night that was ushering in a day like a furnace blast, the hottest July 31 in the history of New York, surely a distinguished day for a child to be born.

While I lay in the hospital bed waiting for morning, I switched on the light and went on reading Dickens's *Great Expectations*. My own expectations, like Philip Pirrip's, were great indeed. They were about to be fulfilled, though the baby I expected, anticipatory itself, had been alive and kicking so long it seemed not much of a transition to make to the world outside.

A boy or a child, I wonder?

In the end Dickens deserved all the credit. This was the right and only book to read, salubrious in effect, following which the miracle was punctually repeated. Next morning at nine o'clock, when I returned to consciousness after the Caesarean and found him born, it was Philip who had taken up existence there. It was Pip himself.

The happiness, overwhelming as before, was the same happiness. B. and I greeted him in speechless welcome, having got what we wanted. As for our forecaster, our prophet, Dr. Caverly still smiled and looked wise. Philip had been a boy all the while, and it was his heart beating, wasn't it?

8

I stayed at home with my children for five years. From time to time I sang them "Hallelujah, I'm a Bum" or "Who's Afraid of the Big, Bad Wolf?" while the Depression gradually lost its grip and lessened. Nobody knew when it came to an end, or whether it ended at all before the Second World War. With Franklin Roosevelt after the spring of 1933, we had the new deal, the new words *relief* and *recovery* for the "forgotten man," though the most eloquent word, the most unnerving, was still *survival*. We were the survivors.

On Christmas Day George V broadcast a message to the world that prosperity was around the corner, and in the following May the Dionne quintuplets were born, plainly a sign of better times. To many, however, the times were sinister; it remained an age of anxiety. What lesson had been learned? Too much was intolerably wrong, too much that Democracy hadn't cured. By now many had turned for answer to Communism; and we Socialists hadn't given up the free man's right to protest.

At least with Prohibition ending in December, 1933, drinking was again licit and lawful. I had grown up under Prohibition. Since I was thirteen years old there had been the wets and the drys, the teetotalers and the bootleggers. Temperance as a reasonable view of life had lost its meaning. So had the pretty word *moonshine*. The voice of indignation had grown shrill as the years passed, with Henry Ford shouting, "Prohibition is here to stay!" and Nicholas Murray Butler crying, "Prohibition must be destroyed!" Amid a general revulsion of feeling, the wets won, the bars opened, and after fourteen years of speakeasies a new kind of drinking parlor was added—the cocktail lounge.

To my chagrin, I couldn't make myself vote for the repeal of the Eighteenth Amendment. I sat embarrassed in the car while B. went bravely to the polling place in the Presbyterian Church and voted like a patriot for the freedom to drink hard liquor—for the end as well of criminal indifference to the law. But lawlessness would never stop. I couldn't rise to welcome back booze and the return of general drunkenness, the neon-lit tavern, the dive, the clip joint with pinball machines. Maybe I yearned for the land of Cockaigne where rivers run red with wine and the people drink their fill of innocent refreshment.

*

Pip was an endearing, blue-eyed child with honey-colored hair. Having two little boys in a cramped apartment meant easily the most humbling days of my life, filled with endless proof of my unfitness, astonishment at being so ignorant, untrained, guilty of too much love and too little intelligence.

At the same time I learned again what love is and the domination of the male—I who had sworn never to marry or have children, had rejected like Thoreau the idea of possessions, had vowed even after marriage to belong to myself, unfettered and in spirit free. The more fool I. Here were two undeniable possessions on my hands, and I loved them and I was not free and I would never be free again.

I felt like the woman described by Chekhov: "If a peasant woman has no troubles she buys a pig." When Grace Musser telephoned one morning during the usual round of catastrophe to ask how I was managing the boys, "They're problem children," I told her truthfully (what did she expect me to say: they're a Pride and a Joy?) "with a problem mother."

"You'll outgrow it, all three," she said.

I meant that Pip was a roarer, a Troubleall, who refused to eat his strained liver for breakfast; that both boys had been exposed to whooping cough; that Dave at nearly three had chewed a whole pad of poisonous safety matches, and ever since Christmas had gone around calling himself Little Lord Jesus.

Yet from the moment Pip was on his feet, they were two of a more rational kind. Pip now had a defender, Dave had a willing slave. One day when I thought they were playing in the back court under our windows, I heard Dave in the front hall weeping aloud in an attempt to calm his shrieking brother and drag him bodily up the stairs. I got them inside the apartment, two figures of grief, before asking what was the matter. Tears splashed down Dave's panicstricken face. He clutched Pip tightly with both arms, while Pip screamed in terror lustier than before.

"What in heaven's name is wrong?" I said.

"A eagle! We saw a eagle!" sobbed Dave. "It's going to eat Pippy up!"

Pip howled afresh at the top of his voice.

"Eagles don't live in New York," I said. "How could you possibly see an eagle?"

"Tommy took us to see it. It was sitting on top of a house, and its eyes get lighted up at night. Tommy said it's going to eat little Pippy!"

"Oh, that," I said. "Pip, stop bellowing for a minute. Listen to me. That's not an eagle. It's an *owl*."

"It's a eagle!" Dave cried. "Tommy said so. Tommy said it was a eagle. It's going to fly down and pow! eat my little brother up!"

"It's a stuffed owl," I said.

Halfway up Loring Place at the Psi U fraternity house, a weathered owl sat perched over the entrance. It wasn't stuffed, I guess, since it had been gilded, but it looked real. At night the shining eyes were lit by electric light bulbs.

I went in haste to the bookcase and picked out two volumes of the *Encyclopaedia Britannica,* eleventh edition, which we had just bought secondhand. Here was a chance to test its efficiency. Sitting between the two boys on the sofa, I opened the first volume to "Eagle." Pip stopped crying straightway at the sight of a book, and David's sobs quieted to an occasional hiccup. They stared obediently at the pictures of the majestic birds, one of them a splendid golden or mountain eagle clinging to a distant peak.

"Now take a good look. And before making up your minds," I said, "what about this?" and I opened the other volume to "Owl." Really, it was a hopeless encyclopedia. The boys leaned forward intent, studying the pictures, one a large hoot owl looking far more savage than the eagle, more ferocious, evil-eyed, and hungry as it tore with its claws at a dead mouse; the other a screech owl, fiercely poised, ready to pounce on its victim like a cruel bird of prey.

"Which bird was it? Which one did you see, boys?" I asked cautiously.

120

At the awful memory they both started to wail again.

"A owl," said David.

*

B. hated to have me spend my evenings writing verse. He would watch in silence with tight lips, or looking up from his book reach over to touch me, scribbling under the lamp, and urge me not to.

"I don't want you to get hurt, my love," he would say.

He was afraid to have me faced with failure. Sooner or later I would despair, finding poetry beyond my powers, or even worse would try to get it published. We used to argue with some heat over this.

"How many good poems are there in the world?" B. would ask. He quoted Montaigne: "A man may play the fool everywhere else, but not in poetry."

"I'm not writing poetry," I would say, patient as with a child. "Verses are made by fools like me."

We were talking of two different things. Mine, I tried to tell him, was a more modest exercise. Poetry was lavish and exalted. "Verse isn't the same thing at all," I said.

"That's only a quibble," he said.

"Especially not light verse," I said. "Light verse is deft maybe and berhymed. It is not moonmad. It aims at agility, not passion. Certainly not at what you call high seriousness."

It aimed at wit, or lightwit, I supposed, which Charles Lamb said was at least as good as aiming at dullness. It seemed to me defensible, an end in itself, as useful a pastime as practicing the piano (we didn't have a piano) or sketching the babies in Fordham Park (I couldn't sketch). It was like trying to grow red roses on the fire escape. One needn't break one's heart.

But B. said it was performance. He said it was communication. "Nobody can be satisfied to stay an amateur, writing for himself. One writes for others, and the single reason for using words is to say something. The single reason for saying something is to be heard."

I mentioned Emily Dickinson, and we both laughed. I asked if he would like to hear me recite my small collection, or say a triolet, but he shook his head and returned to his book.

I knew it was a bore for him to have a wife who "wrote," or wanted to write. Still and all, the thing I was up to seemed fairly harmless. A verse is a verse. Mine were only a kind of notation. The habit of notetaking, an old and private one with me, went back to college days at the University of Chicago when, like Hudibras, I learned to take note, "Transcribe, collect, translate and quote." I began copying down powerful and enlightened words wherever I found them, calling the first notebook "Chiefly about Life." It was the beginning of my education.

"When found, make a note of," said Captain Cuttle in *Dombey and Son*. "Overhaul the wollume, and there find it. . . . When found, turn the leaf down."

Like Montaigne I was creating a memory on paper. Montaigne said he possessed no memory at all but was obliged to write down whatever he wanted available by tomorrow morning. As a young man he wore thick mustaches to help him recall whom he had kissed the night before. The memory clung discreetly for days, giving off a haunting fragrance. It smote him through the nose. But as he grew older, words not whiskers had to suffice.

In graduate school at Columbia, this habit of mine had paid off. Quotations in my notebook, laudable and ripe, were ready when I needed them to please and overpower B.—who never kept a notebook in his life or wore a mustache either, because he didn't have to. His memory was stocked with plenty of passionate items to woo me by. (It contained a number of odd statistics as well, such as "What is the rectal temperature of a hibernating bear?" Answer: 80 degrees.)

Writing a verse meant taking a note and shaping it a little for safekeeping. If the verse turned out ill, the quotation it sprang from was too good to leave around gathering dust. I felt obliged to rescue personally from oblivion such immortal words, to act as it were their advocate—for example, Aunt Mary Emerson's imperious command: "Be still. I want to hear the men talk." Or Thoreau saying: "Do what you love. Pursue your life." Or Fontenelle: *"Quelque fois j'ai dit ha ha."* Or Cummings:

Humanity i love you because you
are perpetually putting the secret of
life in your pants and forgetting
it's there and sitting down

on it

(Cummings said in the same poem, "Humanity i hate you," but I saw no reason for making a note of that.)

I collected words strictly for the virtue in them, like *mealymouth* and *gallipot;* rotund phrases like "the rumble of the tumbrils," "the epistles of the apostles," *un coup de pied dans le derrière;* noteworthy and rhythmic facts like "Swallows have twelve feathers in the tail," "A leprechaun avoids your eye," "Oysters change sex," "Thirty-six square miles make a township," "A tanager eats honeybees," "Lack of teeth is a sign of old age in lions."

Across one end of my driver's license was scratched in pencil: "How do you know that the planet Mars isn't carried around by an angel?" It was said by J. B. S. Haldane, who unfortunately didn't provide the answer.

B. had no need to worry, I would never be a poet. My words would not butter a parsnip or make tigers tame. I

123

would utter no impassioned cry from the heart, speak no tragic confession, reveal no universal meaning. The disasters and folly of the world, the lunacy of man, needed no memorandum from me. One had to be born a poet, even a minor poet.

Yeats said, "People do not invent. They remember." And, as everyone knows, memory deceives. Yet without the power of invention or the imagination of a poet, I would not fabricate or invent: I would remember. I would be a notetaker and remember the notes. Moreover I would remember only what I wanted to, without sadness in it, and not be a preserver of grief. Who would want a memory without a compartment for forgetting?

*

The notebooks also came in handy, in lieu of a diary or journal, for jotting down a biographical fact of special charm or significance. During 1935 three such personal notes appeared, each with a ring of pride to it. Philip, age two, could count to seven. David, age four, had composed a moonpoem:

The moonlight
Shining persons in the night

and B. had finally taken his orals at Columbia for the doctor's degree.

I well recall that woeful day. It had been eight years since B. entered graduate school, eight long years of interruptions to his career, such as courtship and marriage, earning a living, a near-fatal illness, the Depression, and the birth of two children. A pardonable delay. Now at last he had reached the climax, the final testing of his accumulated knowledge.

On the day of his orals I walked the floor of the apartment, scared to death, waiting. What would we do if he failed now? He would be too proud to go on with college teaching with no hope of advancement. How at thirty-five could he start over again? I believed in the brilliance of his mind, in his store of learning, but what fool questions would they ask? A man could know what's what, he could understand the Perpendicular Style and the quantum theory, yet hardly know *everything*. Besides, it was true, B. was unabashed, a hopeless optimist. He was a rejoicer, not a hellgazer like me. Perhaps he hadn't worried enough, trusting too much to the quickness of his wits and his phenomenal memory, to being able to think fast on his feet.

When he took the language tests the year before, preliminary to these orals, he had asked to be examined in all three languages on the same day—Latin, French, and German. Nobody had done that before. The examiners advised against such a reckless stunt. But he liked taking chances, showing what he could do, winning with the odds against him.

Not I. If this examination was not an ordeal to B., it unquestionably was to his wife. I wrung my hands at the hour of trial, imagining him before the board of professors, each a specialist in his field, able (and sometimes glad) to make a monkey out of a candidate. His mind might go vacant, it happened now and then. He might burst into tears, faint away, disgrace himself. He might even leave me afterward.

As in a hospital waiting room, for three hours I walked the floor and sweated. Then the telephone rang.

"Hello, darling," B. said quietly.

"Tell me!" I gasped. "Yes or no?"

"How would you like to go to England this summer?"

So that was it, he had failed. He was breaking the news

125

gently—he wanted to get out of the country, disappear, try to forget. His life was ruined. I held on to the phone, wondering bleakly what to say.

"Will you go with me?" he asked.

"Sure."

"I have to work in the British Museum. There's the thesis still to finish, you know."

"You passed then? You mean you actually *passed?*"

"Of course I passed. God Almighty, what did you expect?"

9

I was thirty years old in the summer of 1936. The trip to England was I figured my farewell to youth, my last fling, the passing of my prime. Jules Renard wrote in his *Journal* in 1894: "Thirty years old! Now I am sure that I shall not escape death. . . . The thought that I am thirty breaks my heart."

It broke my heart more nearly to leave my children behind. B. made the decision. He had three married sisters living in Ohio in towns not far apart, who, it occurred to him, might between them be trusted to look after our boys for two or three months that summer. Margaret, the youngest sister, eagerly agreed to take them. She and Hunter, her husband, with no children of their own, lived in a farmhouse outside Coshocton, Ohio, a few miles from the rest of the family—aunts, uncles, cousins, grandparents—the lot, since no Bevington except B. ever willingly left the state of his birth. The only flaw in the plan was that it meant forsaking a boy of three and a boy of five whose lives were my life, from whom I had never before been separated.

I took them out on the train in June, and it was like delivering the little Princes to the Tower. After a miserable day spent with Margaret and Hunter, during which they underwent my blackest scrutiny, I had to admit their competence. Margaret would make a good mother, at least for two months. She had a calm patience and a warm heart. She would give them affection of a placid sort and more spit and polish than they were used to. Hunter alarmed me mightily. I have seldom met a nicer man, the person without guile whom a child adores and trusts on the spot. He would win them away from me, turn them into contented Ohio-Americans like himself, give them his love and take all of theirs, and I would never get them back whole again.

On a bright grieving day I left them, the apples of my heart, while they held tight to Hunter's hand and saw me go without a squall, a tear, or a second look. I came limping home to New York alone. Beloved as they were, I must go where B. went. We had our boxlike apartment to empty and vacate, for to save money we were putting our goods in storage. I sold my Royal typewriter, and B. sold, alas, the little Whippet. This time it was a wrench to give up the possessions. They had begun to look like the amenities of life.

*

We sailed on June 5 on the *Statendam*, taking along Karl Marx, Queen Victoria (*Leaves from the Journal of Our Life in the Highlands*), and my mother. This last was a mistake, for I doubt that my mother enjoyed any part of the trip. It was too strange, requiring of her too much adjustment; she only relished having been. When the strain was over and she had got safely home, she improved upon her travels and lived in a golden version of them for the rest of her life.

Yet she wanted to go. She thought of herself as a seasoned traveler (most people do), tolerant of other worlds, other peoples. She called herself English by birthright and drank tea for breakfast, though her membership in the D.A.R. was gained through an ancestor named John Raymond who had reportedly been killed at Lexington "in a cowardly and brutal manner" by the British. The one friend she made on shipboard, Miss Fenton of Boston, a maiden lady, showed the same ambivalence—a complacent pride in the English cousins she was on her way to visit and a tendency to talk spiritedly about the Boston Massacre.

The friends B. and I made were less proper than Miss Fenton, decidedly not pro-British. In the third class beaming Dutch people elbowed about whom I admired as fine, respectable Protestant folk, the salt of the earth, some of them American citizens, some not. We bowed to each other with nothing to say. Our constant companions for the voyage—at meals, in the swimming pool, on the dance floor, on deck at night where we walked and argued for hours after the ship was quiet—were of a more disreputable sort. They were a group of Communists and fellow travelers, extreme left-wing radicals, devout and dedicated Marxists, whom after thirty years I feel obliged to protect by using only their first names.

They were quite young, our age or younger, most of them teachers, unmarried, traveling alone. Only Boris was Russian-born. Boris was a theoretical physicist at a midwestern American university, whose table was shoved up so close to ours in the dining saloon that inevitably, the first night at dinner, we fell into conversation. The same evening he introduced us to the others: Bill, who wrote inflammatory articles for the *New Masses;* Judd, on his way to teach history at the American University at Cairo; Grace and

Marianne, two sisters who taught school in California. I don't know how many of them were card-carrying members of the Party, or whether any of them were. It was something they didn't divulge. But one thing was true. Comrade, they were *loyal*. They had undergone conversion. They were committed to the brotherhood of man.

Boris talked all the time, a breastbeater, a geyser, the most articulate, thoroughly indoctrinated and idealistic of the group—a Marxist and Leninist who wanted to save the world. For him the society of capitalist imperialists had failed, was on its rapid way out, finished, doomed, as the Depression had proved. Waving the red flag, he demanded no halfway measure, not a socialized state but a communist state, a classless society. This was the future, he said. Communism was the remedy, the clean break, the escape from world disaster to peace and equality for all.

To Bill, art presented the means by which to teach this beautiful new faith. Art meant no more than propaganda for the masses, for whom the new literary form was "proletarian realism" (about unemployed miners, sharecroppers, factory hands, or taxi drivers on strike). A writer used words to spread the Word. The only good novel was a proletarian novel by Albert Maltz or Albert Halper. The only good play was "Waiting for Lefty." Bill offered me a job writing for the *New Masses,* and one night after several beers he wrote out a glowing letter of introduction to his editor, Joseph Freeman. It said I would be useful to the Cause. Maybe I might have been, I don't know, I never found out.

Judd put his faith in world Revolution, in the class struggle, which had to come, which *was* coming any day now, he said. It would be a war fought for world unity, a people's crusade, won by us internationalists. It had, in fact, already begun. Look for an early bloody uprising in Spain, he told us in whispers.

Grace and Marianne were intense partisans but fairly

inarticulate. They hurried down each night from first class (a conspiratorial gesture in itself) to listen enrapt and agree, twittering away in mild lunacy—two charming girls, well-bred, well-dressed, well-to-do, quite unaware of any irony in traveling in capitalist luxury while they plotted the rise of the proletariat. They were what you call sympathizers.

As Lincoln Steffens said, "All roads lead to Moscow." But not for B. they didn't, not that glory road, oh no! B. emerged, after all, not a schoolteacher Communist or red intellectual. To my astonishment, he stayed unconverted, the sole member of the company who argued stubbornly against their pat answers, fought them, and denied any virtue in the holy Cause. Striving to educate and save him, the others talked loudly on, paying him no heed, unmoved by his explosive attack. His pink liberalism was too conservative and stuffy, too bourgeois. But he found their radicalism worse, shrill and overwrought, singletracked and bloody-minded. What left-wing sympathies he may have had before this journey he lost in anger at their blind ideology. They were drunk and reeling with the new belief. They saw Communism not as disloyalty but as religion, an intelligent choice of gods, the only ransom for mankind. How could one be caught in a net like that?

"*What* revolution?" he would shout. "Another Russian revolution? Is that what you want? *What* world do you want to destroy?"

We had to shush him lest he be overheard. I was embarrassed by the racket he made. He sounded like a rock-ribbed Republican defending private enterprise. He missed the whole spirit of the occasion.

Yet more often than not the talk struck me as deadly, even stupefying. It went on and on, prating social significance, following the Party line, tiresomely longwinded. Boris was a zealot, an agitator, a Mr. Zeal-of-the-Land Busy.

Then at last he managed to anger me also by his endless

131

analyses and solutions, though for a wonder this time he wasn't talking about the working classes but about me. One night as we were dancing together on deck to the ship's orchestra, he gazed long into my eyes.

"Do you want to know what's wrong with you, what your real emotional problem is?" he remarked dreamily. "I've finally figured it out. Shall I tell you?"

"No," I said.

"You want to be a man."

If he had said, "You want to be a Communist," I wouldn't have been so taken by surprise. He would have meant it as a delicate compliment.

"Why do I?" I asked. "What makes you think so?"

"You aren't satisfied to be a female, that's all."

I could have slapped him. Instead of telling him off, I walked away and stared in fury at the sea. After thirty, Max Beerbohm said, one should quarrel with no man, though he didn't say one shouldn't spit in his face. From that night on, I avoided Boris and his hysterical tirades as studiously as possible. He was a vulgar, opinionated young man with highly offensive manners. He was no prize at any university. And his talk was flapdoodle.

*

In London we stayed at the Shelbourne near Russell Square, a shabby little hotel in, as they say, the heart of Bloomsbury. It disappeared in the bombings of World War II and made a hole in the ground. But I haven't unlearned the look of our large threadbare room or the sound of churchbells from nearby Christ Church, Woburn Square, performing "God Save the King" on the quarter hour.

B. and I worked in the British Museum. After a brief guided tour of the Reading Room, during which an attendant told me there were fifty-five miles of books spiraling toward heaven in that vast library, they couldn't keep me out. B. had obtained a card of admission and was safe inside, but he helped me apply also as a "visiting American scholar." Since I had to tell them what I wanted to do in there besides read the books, my hastily improvised research project became "The Sentimental Novel in the Eighteenth Century." I was impressed by its gravity. Each morning I went with him past the iron railings, the pigeons, the fat fluted pillars, and presenting my own card at the door, a Reader now, read till noon the novels of Mrs. Inchbald and Clara Reeve, sitting once or twice in Seat G7 where Karl Marx sat to write *Das Kapital*.

It was a noble room, the greatest library in the world, full of dusty scholars, drudges, and fanatics. Karl Marx worked there daily for thirty-five years in the deepest obscurity, suffered to remain and be ignored. Samuel Butler translated the *Iliad* and the *Odyssey* into prose somewhere in that circular expanse under the dome, discovering in the attempt that Homer was an authoress. B. told me about George Gissing, how he used to strip to the waist and take a bath in the men's washroom, since he lacked the amenity of running water where he lived. Finally a discreet sign appeared: "These basins are for casual ablutions only."

After a lunch at Paggioli's in Soho, of minestrone, wine, and huge strawberries, B. returned to his desk at the Museum while I devoted the afternoon to my mother, in a manner of speaking. I dragged her all over London to gaze at literary sites, shrines, tombs, and monuments, for which she cared not a button. Virginia Woolf said once, "I am a lover of unfrequented shrines," but I loved them unfrequented or even nonexistent, so long as a blue plaque or tablet revealed a writer born on the spot, schooled, married, domiciled, drunk at a tavern, dead, buried, or otherwise memorialized.

I loved the peripheral, the fringes of literature. It seemed a momentous thing to discover Sir Thomas More born on

Milk Street, Milton on Bread Street, the Brownings married in Marylebone Church, Dr. Johnson living at 17 Gough Square and dying at Bolt Court. Carlyle's house, 24 Cheyne Row, Chelsea, had a spare bedroom where Emerson slept, a basement kitchen where Tennyson and Carlyle sat and smoked in silence. Even in Hyde Park Harriet Shelley had drowned herself in the Serpentine. We followed Pepys around London from All Hallows, Barking, from whose tower he watched the great fire, to Seething Lane where he loved his wife, poor wretch, to St. Olave's Church where both lie buried. At the site of Izaak Walton's ironmonger's shop, 125 Chancery Lane, I caught my mother gazing not in awe at the marker but wistfully into the shop window of yarns and embroidery cottons. After that I took her shopping to a Woolworth 3d and 6d, and to Selfridge's on Oxford Street for an American "hot dog in roll" and a chocolate soda.

In 1936 Edward VIII was King. On the morning of June 23, B. and I left our books to watch the ceremony of Trooping the Colour in honor of His Majesty's birthday. We saw him ride along Whitehall to the Horse Guards Parade at the head of his jingling troops, his brothers York, Gloucester, and Kent behind him. Now forty-two years old, he looked more stern and properly majestic under his busby than the debonair young Prince of Wales I had howled to welcome ten years before with the rest of the student body at the University of Chicago. Inside the Parade Ground while the bands played, a man in uniform standing beside us introduced himself as an aviator who had often flown with the King.

"She is here today, you know, your countrywoman," he said. "Over there, I suppose, in the tiered seats—"

"Who is *she?*" we asked.

"Mrs. Wallis Simpson."

So that was her name. Like everyone else we had heard

of the royal romance, the bachelor King hopelessly in love
with a married woman. He must have wooed her that day by
the glitter of his performance, the pomp, the flourish in her
praise. Six months later after nearly toppling the throne, he
would abdicate for her sake and become plain David Windsor.

Our minds full of such royal scandal, we saw another
drama that night, *Henry VIII,* in the open-air theater at
Regent's Park. And it seemed regally seasonable—after the
execution of the Duke of Buckingham, the disgrace and fall
of Queen Katharine, the amorous rise of Anne Bullen, the
death of Wolsey—to stand at attention for still another
spirited playing of "God Save the King." God save royalty.

*

But in my head was the desolation, in the pit of my
stomach the misery, caused by the separation from my children. We had had no word since I left them in Ohio a
month ago—the sound of nothing. B. wouldn't let me send
a cable. Then on July 4, a day meaningless to the English
but skyrockets to me, a thick envelope came with news and
love—love but no longing from two boys abandoned by
their parents. Why did I want them to *miss* me? David had
printed his greeting in one brisk sentence: "We smell skunk
almost every night." Hunter had taken down what Pip had
uppermost in his mind: "The turkey gobbler don't scare
me. I chuck out my muscle and he runs away."

I turned to B. in tears. "Don't you see what's happened?
In only one month he's speaking pure Ohioese."

Hunter ended ominously: "They seem a part of us now."

*

B. found a friendly tobacconist on Great Russell Street
whom he stopped in to talk to every day. B. wanted to know,
among other things, about the British labor movement. He

was pleased to air his own views on John L. Lewis and organized labor in America, the C.I.O. and A.F. of L., in return for the tobacconist's lively account of trade unionism in England. This exchange led B. to ask about the plight of the workers in Spain, of which he had been able to learn nothing from the London newspapers.

"There's trouble brewing all right," he was told. "No doubt about it. And it's coming soon."

Why the conspiracy of silence, the hands-off policy, of the English press? B. had taken the trouble to visit Marx House, hoping to ask questions, but he had been rebuffed. No, there was nobody with whom B. might speak. No meetings were scheduled, no speeches, and, too bad, the clerk added curtly, no garden parties. He left with a few leaflets she handed him.

The tobacconist was more obliging. One morning when B. dropped in as usual, he said, "I think I have something lined up for you," and picking up the telephone called the office of the Transport Workers' Union and asked for Ben Tillett's secretary. The date was July 7.

"I've a gentleman here from America," he said, "interested in the labor movement, friend to labor, friend to peace. He wants to find out what's going on. Can you get him into the meeting tonight?"

"My wife too," B. said.

"Frightfully sorry, not a ticket to be had," said the secretary. "We're expecting a tremendous turnout. But wait a minute, send him over anyway. I can't promise anything but I'll try. Tell him and his lady to meet me here at 7:30, and they can go along with me. It's just possible I can get them in."

The meeting was the International Trades Union Congress, to be held at the Friends Meeting House in Euston Road, a great mass meeting on the subject of "Democracy and Fascism." The main speaker would be Largo Caballero, General Secretary of the Union of Workers in Spain.

When B. and I arrived on the dot at Transport House that night, the secretary waited at the door, a small, black-haired, sallow young man in a bad state of nerves, quivering with excitement.

"I have simply an extraordinary surprise for you!" he said with a gasp, wringing our hands. "It's a stroke of luck, quite unlooked-for. At the very last minute, you see, he suddenly appeared, just popped in. I was the only one here to greet him."

We looked expectant.

"You're going to attend the meeting tonight with none other than Tom Mann!"

B. showed appropriate shock and I smiled brightly. When the young man left to escort his guest from an inner office, I turned to B. in haste.

"Who in the world is Tom Mann?" I whispered.

"English labor leader," B. said under his breath. "Led the great dock strike of 1889. Must be doddering by now. Tell you later."

It was incredible how B. knew these things. Tom Mann, he told me afterward, was a revolutionary who had spent a lifetime as a trade unionist fighting for the working classes. He had led the historic Dock Workers' Strike with Ben Tillett and John Burns. England had imprisoned him twice. An old-line Socialist, he had changed his political allegiance several times, at last to become a member of the Communist Party and a founder of the Party in Britain. One thing he had never been tempted to become was a capitalist. He had stayed devout in loyalty to the workers throughout his long life.

The stout old man who now walked slowly towards us was eighty years old, a hearty man in spectacles with a white mustache and rosy, benign face. I found him charming, especially when he bowed from the waist and gallantly took my arm. "My dear, my pretty dear," he said. "I am honored by your company tonight. Let us go forth together."

"I haven't a ticket," I said.

"Neither have I," said Tom Mann. "Shall we storm the place and demand the right to be admitted?"

At eight o'clock we entered the door of the Friends Meeting House and walked unchallenged straight down the center aisle, B. and I on either side of the old gentleman. Immediately there was a stir; then wildly excited cheers and shouts came from all over the huge auditorium. "Tom Mann! It's *Tom! Tom Mann!*" they yelled and, applauding, the entire audience rose to its feet. Many raised their right arm and clenched fist in the Communist salute.

The ushers tried to escort him to a place of honor on the speakers' platform, but twice he shook his head. They led us up a few steps to a reserved section at the left of the platform where we sat facing the audience. At once the meeting began, everyone again on his feet singing lustily. I looked in doubt from Ben Tillett himself on one side of me to Tom Mann on the other, who smiling his joy pointed to my program where the words appeared of the "Internationale." And I joined in with the rest:

Arise! ye prisoners of starvation,
Arise, ye wretched of the earth.

Arise to unite the human race. Jouhaux spoke that night for France, Mertens for Belgium, George Hicks, M.P. (a weak sister) for England. But it was Caballero the crowd had come to hear. He too was a Socialist, one who, as the program tactfully put it, had "fought for the reform of the Party on Marxian lines." Since the year before, 1935, the Communist Party had promoted the idea of the Popular

Front to unite in a common cause all the enemies of Fascism.

Caballero told the people what they wanted to know—when the Revolution was coming to Spain. A large man slow of speech, he grew loud in anger, shouting with fevered intensity as he pleaded for a united front—an amity of nations to fight Fascism and prevent the certainty of a world war, an infamous second world war. It was the only way left, he cried out in anguish: to *unite,* against the Falangists and other right-wingers who wanted to destroy the government of the people; against the dictators—Hitler, Mussolini, and their powerful little ally, Generalissimo Franco. The Spanish cause was the cause of Democracy against Fascism, the shared foe. The mortal struggle would begin in Spain, he said, a war against war and Fascism. It would start within the next two weeks.

In fact the Spanish Civil War began only ten days later with an uprising of Spanish garrisons in Morocco. The real fighting occurred next day in Madrid on July 18, and all the bullfights were canceled. For the next three years it raged on, in what was after all only a tragic prelude to World War II.

*

Rain fell every day that summer, till the green grass in Green Park looked bought by the yard. The bloom was on Bloomsbury Square. I loved London with a passion—the pubs, churchbells, chimneypots, Englishmen in queues—a love so real that B. took me for a first ride in an airplane (or aeroplane then) to see its spacious extent, a twenty-minute joyride for 7/6 from Croydon circling over the city. Our pilot was an "ace," having downed at least five enemy planes in World War I, a comforting hero to fly with on a windy day as we bumped and swooped along all but flapping our wings.

139

"Did you like it?" B. asked when we landed.

"Umhum."

"Then why did you close your eyes?"

"I looked down and saw John Donne in a winding sheet," I said.

"By God, so did I," he said. "In St. Paul's, the effigy of John Donne. I saw him plain."

*

We paid a social call on Jeremy Bentham one afternoon at the University of London, rather like a visit to Apollo and the Delphic Oracle. An obliging office clerk trundled him out of a closet, where he sat in a glass cabinet on wheels, and left us alone to commune with him in the reception room.

Jeremy Bentham died in 1832 at the age of 84, which made him now 188 years old. Yet here he was, a sprightly gentleman and philosopher, his genial waxen face beaming under a large beaver hat, a musty black suit covering his skeleton, his mummified head at his feet. What a lovable man. Leaning graciously forward with one gloved hand on his cane, he looked ready for a good heart-to-heart talk on pleasure, say, and the pursuit of happiness. I wanted to ask him why he had willed his person as a bequest to University College, but it wasn't necessary. I knew the answer. Jeremy Bentham was by love attached to this mortal world and he didn't want to leave it. Besides, he genuinely liked to make people happy, as he made me happy that day to see him fleshly and immortal, his manner still charitable, surviving his own extinction so well.

*

For the last three weeks we left London and rode on local buses over England, Scotland, and Wales, while my mother traveled on the Royal Scot to Edinburgh and back since she was in the railroading business. She admitted to being tired to death of our literary pilgrimages.

They weren't all literary. Oxford was full of Oxford Groupers or Buchmanites, who mistaking us for one of their pious selves stopped us on the street to inquire, "Are you up for the Groups?" Their aim was Moral Rearmament, a new social order "under the control of the spirit of God." By coincidence we had ridden up in a bus with another Group dedicated to Moral Rearmament and a new social order under the control of Hitler, a strident crowd of Sir Oswald Mosley's Fascist Black Shirts.

Yet Oxford had its gray spires and Christ Church bells, its water-soaked Sophocles found in Shelley's hand when he drowned in the Gulf of Spezia. Outside the Clarendon we ran into an American movie star, Richard Barthelmess of the old silent films.

"Hello, America," he called out, winking at me as he passed.

"Oh, *hello!*" I said, breathing hard.

B. turned around to stare in amazement at him. "Do you know that man?" he asked suspiciously.

"I used to be madly in love with him," I said. "My first love."

Cambridge had its wonderful Pepys' library, which he bequeathed to his college, Magdalene. Three thousand books, that was the number Pepys regarded as the correct size for a gentleman's library, though gentlemen then and now have got along with less. These he had catalogued "according to heighth" from 1 (the smallest) to 3000 (the largest) and placed in twelve carved-oak bookcases—Pepys the orderly man, literate and neat, the booklover, who chose to surround himself with such quietly tasteful objects.

A volume of the *Diary,* bound in leather to match the rest, lay open to the entry for September 6, 1666: his account in cipher of the dreadful London fire that nearly destroyed his world, his house, his books. A second volume was turned to the last page of the diary, his leave-taking to himself: "And thus ends all that I doubt I shall ever be able to do— God prepare me! S.P. May 31, 1669."

As I stared about me, the librarian approached with an offer to come to my aid, inquiring kindly, "Is there something you are looking for?"

There must have been. It would be hard to say in words what, but anyway it was there. I found it.

*

We saw piles of coal at Newcastle, and at Durham the tomb of the Venerable Bede. We walked along the Wye valley above Tintern Abbey quoting Wordsworth, "The still, sad music of humanity," and at Grasmere, across the road from Dove Cottage, discovered a campaign poster that said "Vote for Alf Landon."

But the most literary moment of the summer occurred at the Cataract of Lodore in the Lake Country. In pouring rain B. and I walked one morning the six miles from Keswick to misty Derwentwater, then on through drizzle and muddy paths to Lodore—where the Hotel Lodore effectually hid the little mountain waterfall and was charging the tourists twopence to pass through a turnstile to view it. We were the only tourists.

Owing to the rains, the water (usually a mere brook) came racing down the hillside more or less fancifully as Southey had described it. And there B., the Romantic-Victorian scholar, stood addled by the sight. Without delay he climbed out to the slippery rocks in the middle of the dashing stream and began to recite the opening lines:

> *How does the water*
> *Come down at Lodore?*

At that he lost his footing, slid abruptly off the rock, and began to descend on the seat of his pants, "helter skelter, hurry scurry," in the manner of those tumbling waters. Shouting as he came, he spoke not Southey's words but in the style of Southey, full of unstifled sound and ceremony.

Since it was Pip's third birthday, July 31, I wrote him a verse to give him the general picture: "How did your father come down at Lodore?" He came thundering down, I said. From perilous slipping he came grabbing and gripping, heaving and cleaving, with blasphemous roar:

> *The view was augmented*
> *By words he invented*
> *For water descending*
> *As downward he bore.*
> *Where Southey's endeavor*
> *Took nearly forever,*
> *Your father went farther and yelled a lot more.*

Pip asked us to bring him an icecream cone from England, and in August we sailed home on the *Volendam*. We had been a lifetime away. In my heartsickness to see the boys I wept into the Atlantic, raising the level of the ocean, B. said, increasing its amount of salt.

10

David went in the fall to Public School No. 91, where he was squeezed with fifty children into a one-room kindergarten. During the single month of his attendance, he received A for conduct, probably for learning how to behave like a sardine. The one time I visited his class he sat staring trancelike into space, waiting his turn at whatever group activity like milling around the room the harassed teacher could devise. He was lost at school, to which he had looked forward; limp among too many children. Yet on a September day of Yom Kippur, when Pip and I took him as far as the schoolyard, there was nobody at all. A little boy who attended the kindergarten met us on the sidewalk as we gave up and started home. He was strolling past dressed in his best clothes.

"What's the matter, David?" he asked. "Aren't you an American?"

Much as B. and I believed in public-school education, we were beaten by numbers. But when I suggested a private school as a last resort, B. hit the ceiling.

"I won't have him in a private school among snobs!" he shouted. "I won't have him growing up segregated!"

The result was that I went to work for a private school, the Barnard School for Boys at the north end of the Bronx. Overnight the pattern of our life changed. Pip, age three, was enrolled in the nursery school and both boys were riding back and forth on the Barnard School bus, carrying their lunchboxes. Pip hated every kind of sandwich I made him, gagging at cheese, but he gladly accompanied David into the wide world as a schoolboy.

The beauty of Barnard was its small classes, eight or ten to a group. Yet ironically the headmaster hired me to bring in more students, to ring doorbells and invite people living in the vicinity to send us their boy. The owner of a local shoestore grudgingly permitted me to go through his files to track down parents of male children shod at his store. As leads they proved one hundred percent bad. These were lean years for selling, and the least of my talents was salesmanship. I walked the streets in a cold sweat, too cowardly to approach the house to sell my product. If a maid shooed me from the door, I apologized and crept off, feeling despised and rejected for the rest of the day. In three months only one housewife invited me inside.

"Come on in," she cried, with open arms. "You're just the person I want to see."

She led me weak with gratitude to her bedroom, where she was trying on dresses on approval from Best's and wanted my opinion of their fit. Her boy attended the Fieldston School, to which in a model sales pitch she eloquently bent my ear urging me to send mine. Out of pure cowardice I said I would.

At last Dr. Hazen took me off the road and made me

school librarian, where all I had to learn was the Dewey decimal system. I worked mornings to pay the boys' tuition, and only once was I reprimanded by the headmaster and almost fired. On that day David came down with mumps at 9:00 A.M. on arrival at school, after showing no visible swelling at breakfast. Dr. Hazen blamed me for exposing the children of paying customers, who naturally demanded for the price that the place be kept free of germs. David had peppered the son of Edward J. Flynn, the Democratic boss of the Bronx.

It was an excellent school, neither experimental, progressive, permissive, nor child-centered, where the boys thrived. By unruffled methods it gave them a taste for learning that led them eventually to become college professors, and Mlle. Boucher taught them a little French. Like their father they were bright, one-tracked, and absentminded. When David learned to write, he used to send himself notes to remind him what not to forget: "Notice. Dear David, dont forget to eat lunch. David." The bus driver told me he checked to make sure the Bevington boys started home with their pants on. They left behind coats, caps, shoes, lunchboxes, and each other.

I said, "I live with three like that."

I expected B. to run into me some day on a New York street and inquire, "I beg your pardon, haven't we met before?" Yet every night of his life he asked, "Did I forget to tell you today that I love you?"

*

I worked afternoons at New York University, directly across the street from our apartment house on upper Loring Place. Brown House (since torn down and demolished) was an elegant pillared mansion built early in the century by the architect Stanford White, later bequeathed to the University as a home for the President, that now housed the

English Department in unaccustomed splendor. Its formal drawing rooms, aglow with red velvet hangings and gilt doodads, were used for serving tea or listening to an occasional poet.

The secretary of Brown House was a blonde divorcée who had been hit by lightning. This experience with inclemency sometime in her mysterious past had apparently done her no harm, it hadn't felled her. On the contrary it was her pride and distinction, a fascinating calamity. *"I've* been struck by lightning!" she announced from time to time, an effective and cowing remark during a thunderstorm. I tried while I worked there to write a verse in her praise, but could think of nothing to say beyond the fact that she was now kin to a tall pine tree or a church steeple.

Belowstairs, in the damp cobwebbed basement of Brown House, a reading library or Browsing Room had been added, the recent gift of an unnamed donor who only stipulated that the place have the familial air of home. It was fitted out with sofas, easy chairs upholstered in imitation leopardskin, floor lamps, coffee tables with ash trays and large volumes of art reproductions—Botticelli, Rembrandt, the sculptures of Rodin—and along the walls a thousand volumes to tempt students to drop in at will and, well, browse.

I was a hostess without teapot (tea was served upstairs by the lightning-bolt secretary to English instructors, not students), a welcomer who talked, if they wanted to talk, about the books in alphabetical order on the shelves. *The Bible Designed To Be Read As Living Literature* stood next to Ambrose Bierce's *Devil's Dictionary*. It was meant to be a gentleman's library (the size of Montaigne's in his tower, one-third the size of Pepys'), chosen by the gentlemen of the English Department to represent their taste and range gracefully through the alphabet: Brillat-Savarin and Boccaccio. Heine, Hippocrates, Horace. Pater, Pepys, Petrarch, Petronius, Pirandello, Poe, Proust. And the works of P. G. Wodehouse. Yet loud was the outcry from the faculty that the students, let loose among these volumes, far from behaving like gentlemen would snore on the sofas, befoul the ash trays, wipe their feet on the leopard-skin furniture, and steal the books. During the years I presided there, nobody slept but me and only one book disappeared—Volume II of Casanova's *Memoirs*. Some book-lover must have found it lovable.

I had read most of the collection before and set myself to read the rest, always glad to do any book that favor. But how much time had I? Montaigne went up a circular staircase of 46 steps to a library of 1000 volumes when he was 38 years old, and there he stayed. I went down 10 steps to the Browsing Room for the afternoon, already aged 31. Besides, the problem soon became acute how to keep awake after lunch. I would gaze drowsily across the room at twenty boys calmly smoking, alert and unwearied as they turned a page in the quiet, then drift off into unconsciousness over my book. When my head hit the desk, nobody laughed except Leslie A. Fiedler, a student then, who wore so early the scornful air of a literary critic.

In desperation I sought a less soothing pastime than reading and once more took up the writing of verse which, I will say this for it, has never put me to sleep. The little room became a refuge, a workshop, *une arrière boutique*. But how much time had I? Charles Wesley had managed to write 9000 poems in his lifetime, averaging 10 lines a day for 50 years. Emily Dickinson wrote 1,775 poems and no hymns.

At least the work brought a taste of glory that I think leaves one wholly self-intoxicated but once. One morning at breakfast I opened the New York *Herald Tribune* to find at the head of F.P.A.'s column "The Conning Tower" a ballade of mine in print. The next thing would be an invitation to lunch at the Algonquin with Dorothy Parker.

"Isn't that my name?" I asked B., handing the paper to him.

He hadn't noticed the verse but he read it now. "It scans," he said, which was high praise. "It sounds like Villon. The wonder is, love, you wrote it instead."

*

John D. Rockefeller died at 97, the richest man in the world, and I don't know what became of his hat. In the same year (the summer of 1937) we went again to the Farm, as we had gone for the past six years without ever buying the little schoolhouse on Bacon Hill. Bobby and Tom Fansler were in Europe, having left their farmhouse and three young daughters in my care. While B. taught the six weeks of summer school at New York University, I lived at Heyshott with five children, theirs and mine, and a Negro woman named Gay Nickens. Then the older girls, Sue and Cyndy Fansler, went to camp and I kept Jill, going on five, for the rest of the summer.

We had our hands brimful, Gay Nickens and I. It was never the summer of a dormouse. All eight children were generally on the premises, counting three from the other farm, ranging in age from Pip, four, to Peter Flanders, eleven. They read a lot in haughty isolation—always someone locked in the one bathroom with *The Bastable Children* or sprawled in the treehouse with *Babar*—till even Pip taught himself to read from the Montgomery Ward catalogue and learned to print his letters: "Dear Jilly I love you do you love me Tell the truh." Jilly on her part made up a marching song for Pip that to one small drum they liked to march to: "Bang the penises, roll the vulvas, ta-ta-ta-ra-siss-boom!"

The older children roamed the hills on the two horses Flora and Judy; the little ones played in orchards and barns, with David astride the roofbeam hanging on by the seat of

149

his pants. They were adorable, willful, untamed children in the wild countryside. When Jill split her foot open at the brook, we rushed her, bloody and undaunted, the ten miles to the nearest doctor. When Pip plummeted out of the swing and knocked himself unconscious by crashing on his head, we drove the same route, ten fearful miles to ask how badly hurt he was. All night I sat beside his bed counting his erratic pulse, marveling how any of us survived being a child, let alone bringing up a passel of antic children.

Gay Nickens was a match for whatever trouble came her way. The only admission she made that life on occasion flummoxed her was to laugh and shake her head, muttering "Don't that beat *all!*" I got in the habit of saying it myself.

I never had a Negro friend before. Yet Gay and I grew to love each other, with a good deal in common. She was ten years older, already a grandmother, but each of us had sons, each had lived in New York through the black years of the Depression. Gay knew the real ferocity of it and the threatening. She had lived in Harlem close to disaster, without a husband who had left her, without work till the Fanslers hired her as their maid. She was wise but untaught. She kept as much love of life as I and was on good terms with it, but she hadn't my luck in being white. The hatred I would have felt, the resentment, Gay refused to learn. The thought crossed my mind that it would take more than Socialism to change the grief of the world and set her free.

Sally was at the other farm to tell us what to do. She drove back and forth between the houses in Winnie, her Model A Ford, and she told us for one thing to learn the three-part *Suscepit Israel* for women's voices from the Bach "Magnificat." We three would give a full-dress performance on the front lawn next weekend to surprise Moll and B.

The idea rocked Gay and simply convulsed her. "What was that song again? 'The Magnificent'? It's a riot! It's the last thing I ever heard!" she cried and held her sides with laughter.

"Sally," I said, "you've met your match at last. Let me see you make Gay sing."

"She'll sing all right, just the way you did," said Sally.

Gay slapped her hand on her knee. "Don't that beat *all?*" she gasped, wiping away the tears. "That'll be the day!"

Anyway we were too busy to sing. Sally was learning to play the recorder, which ravished her as ever it did Pepys. At night her piping echoed across the valley, thin as a pennywhistle, sad as the music of the damned moving in hell to flutes and soft recorders. And I lay in my bed and wept to hear her till she played a wrong note, paused, and like the whippoorwill under the window started the same phrase over again, "Whippoorwill, whippoorwill—"

*

When B. came by train to Canaan on Friday night and I met him in our four-door Windsor (I've never heard of anyone else owning a Windsor), all cares fell away. With a man in the house, a tolerant man but positive in his views of polite behavior ("Goddamn it, Dave, sit down in that car!"), the children were not unruly and no crises arose. We sang in the dooryard with Sally and Moll, carried further along the notes of Palestrina—"*O bone Jesu,*" "*Adoramus te*"—and on Saturday night went up to Pop Gowan's to the barn dance.

We went bringing Gay Nickens and the eight children, who sat along the wooden benches in a clean, sober row. My partner in the dance would be a gent smelling sweetly of cows who never spoke a neighborly word yet led me forth with a thunderous courtesy. A fat farmwife in a billowing skirt would scoop B. off his feet, swing him in the air, whirl him over her head halfway out of his jacket, and set him down gentle as a baby. B. held on, winded but happy in her strong arms.

Dip and dive and do-si-do, circle up four and away we go! The caller and fiddler, a grizzled fellow with a cracked voice, sawed away at "Turkey in the Straw" or "My Darling Nellie Gray," a mug of hard cider within reach.

"Where did you learn to call?" I asked him once between sets, fanning my hot face. "Was it handed down in your family from father to son?"

He grinned and reached into his coat pocket. "Hell, no," he said, "had to pick it up myself out of this here instruction book. All you do is you send off to Sears and Roebuck."

*

I remember a late Sunday afternoon when I counted with sinking heart eighteen unexpected guests in the house for supper. To stretch out the menu, Gay and I searched the cellar, mousing around till we picked out of the mud a few of last year's walnuts to grind up with mayonnaise to make sandwiches. But why, I ask myself, didn't I keep a journal of such hospitality? Why didn't I list daily each visitor and guest we had, each passerby?

It might have helped in the end to know whether Alger and Priscilla Hiss stopped to see us that summer. Whittaker Chambers testified that he saw Alger constantly throughout the year 1937, and Alger said steadfastly that Chambers lied. I might have given him an exact date when his need was desperate, twelve years later. It was a bitter thing to realize I couldn't be sure, I didn't know.

He was there several times during those years, when he and Priscilla would stop on their way to and from a holiday in New England. I see them now arriving at the door, and for a few seconds there is Alger's warm smile, his voice, our delight in greeting him. We hurry forward from whatever we are doing and the curtain falls, in the way memory has of revealing then blacking out a moment. If one clear vision stays, why that and not another? So I go back and back, trying again, "Now, here we stood—" Then what happened?

Alger was a gallant man, mild and considerate, who seemed of course a member of the family. Priscilla was Tommy Fansler's sister. B. and I had known them both for the last six years, though since Alger had gone to Washington to the State Department we had little occasion to see them. Now and then they dropped in at the Farm.

He was different from the rest of us, more strict, with a touch of reserve that made us hesitate to talk loosely or foolishly in his hearing. We used to reflect on this after they had gone.

"Alger's an idealist," Moll said once. "He wouldn't hurt a rabbit. Certainly he wouldn't hurt a man either."

We couldn't parade our politics before him, our liberal leanings, any more than we could before Ralph Flanders, Moll's Republican brother who became a U.S. Senator from Vermont. Alger was in the government. We respected his idealism and his integrity.

But now the past is forever gone as time is gone. And we are gone—all ghosts, as he is, of that lost time. Clearly his dark story, one of the darkest of the 1930's, is beyond my telling. I know too little, no more than that a man's life was tragically sacrificed. Yet it is true that a person doesn't inspire the faith we had in him without reason. When Alger was accused in 1949, it was as if we were accused ourselves: we were on trial, a part of the strange catastrophe. In bewilderment we asked, "What have I done?" Our loyalty too appeared in question. If he was guilty, weren't we all guilty, each to his own degree, each in his way? Wasn't our whole generation?

I think Moll was possibly right. "If Alger is guilty," he said in his bafflement and grief, "then I know nothing whatever of human beings. I can't tell the difference between a good man and a bad. I can't tell one man from another." I believe as Moll did, without courage to hope any longer that the explanation may be easy or even forthcoming, or that there is a simple answer somewhere, a key to the mystery, a solution. The answer lies buried in our own lost time and our deeply frightened world, quick to believe in a man's guilt, ruthless to hound and condemn him. Out of it one thing alone is terribly certain: the harm it did can never be undone. We lived in a blundering world.

It was Montaigne who in his own day deplored the temerity of those who dare to sit in judgment: "After all, it is setting too high a value upon our conjectures to have a man roasted alive for them."

11

W. H. Auden called the 1930's "a low dishonest decade."
But that was after the decade was over—after the Spanish
Civil War had ended in 1939 in total collapse and defeat,
in *nada,* all resistance to Franco destroyed, Spain the bloody
loser. It was after three years of the shocking Moscow purge
trials, which proved in their savagery and betrayal that
Stalin had joined the dictators, rejecting human rights—or
whatever it was Communism had stood for—in favor of
tyranny, showing once and for all that if Fascism was in-
tolerable Communism was equally so. It was after the last
disillusioning blow in August, 1939, of the Russian non-
aggression pact with Hitler. It was after Hitler had seized
Austria and made it a puppet state, after Czechoslovakia
had fallen, after Hitler's march into Poland had led to the
final outbreak of World War II. It was after God knows

how many million Jews had died in German concentration camps. Human beings had no rights after all, not even the right to exist.

Auden called his poem "September 1, 1939," written at the tailend of a terrible decade. By then the words low and dishonest were far too good for it.

The sense of disaster came to us, as it comes to the unknowing, belatedly. Only afterwards did we see where we had been heading as the clock ran, straight to the brink of cataclysm. I think I was seldom conscious of the peril, at least as a threat to my private world, except when I heard Hitler's voice over the radio, screaming and ranting from Berlin, the manic, hysterical voice of a madman. Then I listened in real fear to his frenzied rages, the bluster of a killer. "Germany wishes to live in peace!" screamed Hitler, flinging out his insane defiance. He was stupid enough to destroy the earth.

*

Yet increasingly I was aware of a growing unease about myself, of being harrowed by my own daily events, anxious and insecure, and of hating it. It was my own war of nerves. I was against being harrowed, whether by a book, a newspaper, or an attempt to cross Fordham Road in traffic. I hated to cringe, to be alarmed, distressed, stunned, numb with horror, or frightened to death. People differed from me, I knew, in their capacity to accept from time to time being desolated. They were braver, more sensible in facing life and reflecting that none escape its woe. "I could a tale unfold," cried Hamlet's father, "Would harrow up thy soul, freeze thy young blood." When a friend urged me to see the new Alfred Hitchcock film, The Lady Vanishes, "Is it harrowing?" I asked.

"Oh my, yes!" she replied with relish, pleased to be able to recommend the plot so highly.

It was a question of fortitude. A sign outside a grocery store said, "Are your brakes set?" I wished mine were. With every passing day it seemed harder to accept the harrowing, to bring up my children in this violent, hellbent city. There were too many frayed edges, too many headlines in a hagridden world. And by that much is one diminished. Fear had me by the throat. I was afraid of losing a child in the New York subway, suddenly separated from him by a closing door. I had a recurrent dream of staring at his white face inside the car as the train moved away, leaving me terrorstricken on the station platform.

Wherever we went I had to teach my children fear, warn them about traffic and against strangers, let them learn anxiety. It was a matter of life and death. Pip had run away to seek his fortune at the age of four, and when I finally caught up with him in his bright green sweater, a dozen blocks away at the Grand Concourse, I was speechless. I merely took him by the hand in a tight grip and stumbled back home, careful to obey all traffic lights. The utmost that life could do to me would be to maim or kill my child. But it could do that.

*

Under the heading of light entertainment I led my children forth to be diverted by fear, managing very early to harrow up their souls. David would ask, hopeful as we set out on one of these excursions, "Will it be funny?," but we seldom had such luck. In March, 1938, we attended in their innocence and mine the film *Snow White and the Seven Dwarfs*, and for a while David laughed himself sick at the antics of the Walt Disney clowns. Pip echoed him. I told myself this time we had really made it. Then along came the witch. As always happens, along came the witch.

She threw David into a panic. Tense and frowning, he began to squirm, covering his eyes, peering out in the dark to see if she was still there. Next he crawled hastily from his seat and crouched on the floor, making no sound but shuddering all over like a whipped animal. I felt like a dog. Philip turned to his father, fortunately on hand to protect us, and grabbing his arm quavered, "You said it was a movie, didn't you, Dad?"

After that we rested on our oars until *The Wizard of Oz* came along and scared the pants off them.

I also was harrowed too young. One of the first movies I saw in childhood, *A Fool There Was*, had the vampire Theda Bara in it, who gave me hiccups. I see her now, whitefaced, heavylidded, slinking down a staircase in her black satin gown to reduce a man to a quivering jelly. "Kiss me, my fool," she cried, gazing like a snake into his eyes. Unnerved by this frolic, I burst into tears and, heaving with sorrow, warned and severely lectured to by my mother, staggered up the aisle and, led by her from the theater, bawled the whole length of Main Street on the way home.

"What in the word is wrong with Helen?" people asked in concern, stopping my mother as she pulled me along sodden and blinded by grief.

"Nothing, nothing at all," answered my mother impatiently. "Her stomach is a little upset."

There were the books too in my childhood that strove to sear and appall. Walking through the living room at night, I would skirt the bookcase with dread, knowing well what lurked there. One was a copy of Poe's tales, the chilling murders in the Rue Morgue. One was "The Hound of the Baskervilles," which made me afraid of dogs thereafter and the howling of dogs. A withering book was Rider Haggard's *She,* the tale of the gorgeous Ayesha who, aged two thousand years, ended by shriveling into an unspeakable thing of yellow skin and bones, dwindling into a handful of dust, then into nothing. Oh, oh. Though Rider Haggard wrote a sequel, *Ayesha, the Return of She* (why not of *Her* this time?), I could face no more of that. As for Henry James's "The Turn of the Screw," it shook me for life.

*

I had many qualms about my children's upbringing, doubts and misgivings that certainly B. didn't share. He was not a worrier. His conscience left him at peace. When B.'s father wrote to ask why the boys hadn't been baptized, offering to repair the omission and the sooner the better, I wondered at my stubbornness. B. and I had been brought up in the Methodist Church, partaking of its ceremonials. What harm would it do to agree to this one? Of what heritage was I robbing them? David could give a lucid account of the solar system and the origins of life on this planet, from the first cell evolving into the first ape, yet he asked blankly, "Who is Adam?" He hadn't been inside a church except to an organ recital.

His friend Dickie at the Barnard School, as well as the other children he played with, went to Sunday school.

David said: "Dickie knows the Ten Commandments."

I said: "Do you know them?"

David said: "I don't have to. I'm not a Christian."

They had a go at Christianity at the Christmas season, when first David, then Pip, was chosen to play the part of Joseph in the Barnard School Nativity Scene. The manger had hay in it, a homemade silver star shone above, grouped around Mary and the Baby were infant kings and shepherds, plus a choir of mothers. The year David was Joseph, Pip passed for an angel of the Lord, dressed in a pillowcase, cardboard wings, and tinsel halo. He led in on tiptoe a meek procession of cherubim looking ready to fly, his face utterly without guile—so neat, so neat the optical illusion.

Yet my stubbornness was consistent, all of a piece. I lacked what is called formal or conventional belief, and the fact betrayed me in unexpected places—in a talk with Harmon Chapman, for example, on the subject of the soul. Harmon was a close friend, a professor of philosophy at New York University with whom B. dearly loved to argue. They would yell at each other half the night with affection and respect, in violent disagreement on almost any subject: politics, the meaning of perception, or the teachings of John Wesley. B. might be no longer a Christian but he was still a Methodist. One night in our apartment Harmon leaped waspstung from his chair, shook a finger in B.'s face, and shouted in outrage, "John Wesley is a *patoot!*" Each accepted willingly enough the credentials of the other as a thinker, but the struggle with ideas drove them absolutely crazy.

When I made up my mind during the winter to read straight through the works of Plato, I wanted Harmon to hear of it because he was a Platonist. I thought he would be pleased, and at the outset he was. But when I tackled the *Phaedrus* and ran into a problem, he grew surprisingly concerned. In the *Phaedrus* Plato divides the soul into three parts, having the forms of two horses and a charioteer. You would think one might accept that graceful image, but I couldn't.

"Harmon," I said, "are you ever bored by Plato? I mean the way he keeps harping on the soul. Every time I come to the word *soul* on the page, which is constantly, I have to jump over it."

Harmon's jaw dropped. He looked astounded. "Why?" he said.

"I don't know what *soul* means."

It seemed a harmless enough admission, but the effect

was electric. Harmon wet his lips to speak. He shook his head in bafflement and turned up his eyes in despair.

"What for God's sake are we going to do?" he cried.

"It's nothing," I said. "It's just a word I don't understand. I'm sorry I mentioned it."

"Just a *word!*" he exclaimed. "Helen, this is awful. This is unheard of. It's the absolute limit!"

Hurriedly he offered to save me. He would meet with me one evening a week to do some soul-searching and take me through a refresher course in the history of philosophy. Like Aristotle we would inquire the meaning of the soul, its immortal nature, its harmonious functions, its incorporeal existence. We would evolve a theory of the human soul. I was moved by his concern, but no, I said, no thank you.

"Why not?"

"I don't think I've got a soul."

Harmon groaned. "But of course you have, my dear, like everybody else."

"Well, if so, it's a straying soul, I've lost it. I don't know what it is or where it is. Let's leave the soul to poetry," I said, "where it belongs."

The poet John Donne knew where his soul dwelt, inside his heart:

What if this present were the world's last night?
Marke in my heart, O Soule, where thou dost dwell

It emerged, in *"The Ecstasy,"* to hang suspended in the air " 'twixt her and mee" and in the language of interinanimating love negotiate to become one with the soul of his beloved. Byron's soul, on the other hand, was in his head, "The dome of thought, the palace of the soul." Milton's was in his eyes ("Thy rapt Soul sitting in thine eyes").

161

Yeats's soul went to Byzantium to clap its hands and sing, and John Brown's went marching on. Wordsworth's soul was a rising star, Rilke's a swan, Shelley's an enchanted boat (W. H. Henley's too, apparently, since he was captain of it). Gerard Manley Hopkins's soul alternately sang and drooped like a caged skylark imprisoned in the narrow bonehouse of his body. Andrew Marvell's bird-soul cast the body's vest aside and flew off to greener boughs,

> *Where like a bird it sits and sings,*
> *Then whets and combs its silver wings.*

Oliver Wendell Holmes's soul resembled a shellfish or nautilus that grew a little too lofty for its chambered shell.

So the soul, a hard organ to track down, might become a moth, a dove, or a butterfly. It might be situated in the liver, the midriff, or the pineal gland. It rose to the lips and departed with the last breath. Oh my, what poetry is!

"Come Helen, come give me my soul again."

"I said to my soul, 'Be still'—"

*

In the spring of 1939, the last ominous year of the 1930's, we took the boys for another try at light entertainment to the World's Fair to have a look at the future—the World of Tomorrow.

The mockery of the occasion never dawned on us, or the irony that, since it was David's eighth birthday, May 13, he asked as a treat to see something *really* funny. We saw Democracity. Out of the drained swamp and refuse dump of Flushing Meadows rose up the ideal city of Tomorrow, to be glimpsed briefly from a moving platform while a chorus of a thousand canned voices sang a marching song of jollier days to come.

Democracity looked an intemperate dream, a heaven of

fluorescent lighting and gold plumbing. So did the Futurama of General Motors, which took us to some mechanical paradise of about 1960. We returned then to earth and to please David (by now thoroughly aggrieved) settled for Frank Buck's Jungleland and Billy Rose's Aquacade where 177 pretty girls with Eleanor Holm swam to waltz music.

But what tomorrow actually lay in wait, a few months ahead? Any tomorrow at all? Around the Court of Peace with its Plaza of Light and Rainbow Avenue, the pavilions of twenty-two foreign nations presented a strangely portentous United Front. Russia's building had a colossal figure of a Worker holding up the Red Star. Japan had designed a Liberty Bell of cultured pearls and diamonds. Nazi Germany was altogether missing. Since Hitler had overrun Czechoslovakia in March before the opening of the Fair, the Czech building stood undone, uncompleted. Germany was far too busy to participate in this child's play, preparing ruthlessly every hour for world war and world conquest.

The most prophetic look of Tomorrow, had we but recognized it, was the exhibit of manmade lightning. B. thought the boys would like that, and again we sat as a family harrowed, cringing at the performance, occupying with chattering teeth a ringside seat while ten million volts of lightning were discharged at intervals to the crash of premonitory thunderbolts. Today's man prepared the mind for Tomorrow's man, in his irresistible need to invent the means of his own destruction.

*

On Sunday, September 3, the day England replied to Hitler's march on Poland by declaring war on Germany, we were at the Farm with the Flanderses over the Labor Day weekend. A neighbor ran in on Sunday morning to tell us Neville Chamberlain's announcement over the radio—"This country is at war." We heard but were too appalled to believe. Moll and B. drove at once to Canaan to buy the New York *Times,* a dependable voice of doom. They returned with pale faces, too depressed to do more than nod their heads. For the rest of the day we sat numbly together as if someone had died, smoking, talking in low tones.

It had happened at last, the war against Fascism. The catastrophe would now proceed unhalted. Neutrality was impossible, and America would soon be involved. Our turn would come to reap the wrath from the wrath-bearing tree.

I thought: thank God my husband is too old to be ordered up for killing, my sons are too young. How long is a war—about four years long? They will not die. In this century you had to be born at the right moment in the right place to miss dying in the wars. To survive, you had to strike it on the nose, be either a prewar or postwar person, which many were unable to do. None of us in this serene countryside would be destroyed or take part in destroying. We would manage (the odds were) to slip past another world disaster; we would escape, it wouldn't happen to us—not this time.

Mercifully we had no way of knowing Moll's future part, how far he would be implicated and how responsibly in this global war. More than three years would pass before he was sent by his government on a secret mission to Los Alamos, as mathematician with the project that created the first atomic bomb. The A-bomb was exploded into a mushroom cloud in the red desert at Alamogordo, New Mexico, at dawn on July 16, 1945, and Moll was both witness and participant.

Soon after that mortal event, on his return to New York, he brought me in a matchbox the gift of a tiny piece of glassy radioactive sand fused by the nuclear blast—as a relic, I guess, a memento, a sentimental keepsake, a small souvenir. It was like Moll to be generous with his friends. But he hadn't reckoned on my craven view, nor did I ever enlighten him. The atom bomb was already in my heart. I was aghast to receive this token of it, too suspicious of the inhuman power of these isotopes or gamma rays to keep such a lethal gift around. You couldn't put a deadly thing like that, threatening to your children and all their descendants, on the coffee table. You couldn't drop it casually into the garbage can. Finally I buried it in a flowerpot on the fire escape (where it may still be contaminating the Bronx) and tried to take it off my mind.

Eventually the bomb was to provide a means of bringing an end to World War II—an end to Hiroshima as well, perhaps some day an end to us all, to the whole planet. It was to be a frightful weapon in the war that now, on this warm, peaceful September day in 1939, had so disastrously begun.

*

Auden said in his poem marking that September cataclysm: "We must love one another or die." Earlier in the year I had heard him speak one night at Columbia University, soon after his arrival in America to enter upon his self-imposed exile from England and from war itself. He had taken part on the side of the Loyalists in the Spanish War of Liberation, but it had failed. Whether in disillusionment or despair, he hurriedly bowed out of this one.

His subject that night was "The Poet in a Topsy-Turvy Society." I could have found a stronger adjective for it, less jocular, and so doubtless could he. For he was recommending not only physical but spiritual exile from a sick and chaotic society, a failed world. The poet is a misfit in this world, he said, where mankind is betrayed and the planet doomed. Let him accept his isolation, withdraw, live a life apart and do his work. Let him remain, man and artist, aloof and uninvolved. "Every poet stands alone."

No man is an island, then, unless he happens to be a

poet? But what of the ordinary man in the street (or in the last ditch), I wondered. How was he to meet his new dilemma, now with hate so ready to rule the world? This splendidly rousing line of Auden's poem (shortly to be written come September) must have been meant, after all, just for him, poor helpless Jackself—not for the artist, not for Auden, but for the common man—"We must love one another or die."

And that, so far as I recollect, was the final irony of 1939.

12

By moving to the new apartment house next door, we definitely improved our status and our lot. We moved from lower class up to lower-middle. After the shabby years in dingy, beehive apartment houses with narrow dirty halls and dark-green peeling paint, we emerged hightoned at last into the light. The house on the corner of 183rd Street had a lobby with an oil painting, an elevator, an incinerator, and, dear God, a doorman. Our four-room apartment on the ground floor front contained a sunken living room with, purchased to fit, a secondhand Knabe baby grand.

As usual B. didn't want to improve his lot, especially by acquiring a doorman. "Affectation and display," he said. "Fine airs, false pride, and conspicuous consumption."

"Bigotry and intolerance," I said. I didn't like doormen either, but this one in maroon uniform came with the building. We couldn't boggle at him.

The boys and I had watched from our windows the construction of the building from the excavations up, slowly cutting off our sunlight and view of the treetops. During an attack of chickenpox, the children witnessed with whoops of joy the dynamiting of the solid rock to hollow out its foundations. From then on all winter, one game appealed to them, the drama of demolition, which with its tension and theatrics was performed daily in our living room. While I lay under the broadloom rug, playing the role of the solid rock, David operated the cardboard plunger and Philip waved the red flag.

"Danger!" yelled Pip, running around the room and tramping on me as he ran.

David stood in a corner, hand poised. When the place was clear of pedestrians, *"Fire!"* he shouted and pushed down. The dynamite exploded followed by a rumble and muffled roar as I leaped up under my iron mesh carpet, then subsided choking in the dust into shattered bits and chunks of rubble. I loathed the game, but the children never tired of it.

Before we picked up and moved, Gay Nickens came one afternoon to tea. When she left I impulsively gave her the floor lamp, the wedding gift from Home Study (which she must have lugged all the way home on the subway). For the first time in nearly twelve years of marriage I prepared to keep house without this faithful piece. It was still unbruised and beautiful, with onyx base and genuine parchment shade, and I loved it. I would like to believe I gave it to her out of love. The probable truth is that the Knabe piano and the doorman had worn away my defenses. More possessions meant something more to be possessed by. Thoreau still monitored my mind, prompting me to lighten the load. Maybe it was a purification ceremony.

B. took it hard to lose a floor lamp and gain a doorman. His worldly goods were disappearing too fast to suit him.

No sooner were we settled in our quarters than he found a new threat—the incinerator. He began to miss things, or thought he did, which could only have disappeared because I had burned them up. This obsession made us both edgy, and I wasted precious hours in a frantic search for whatever he had misplaced and believed already in flames.

"I just want to hold on to the pieces," he would say when I handed over his cuff links.

I said he might have a little more faith in me, since anyway I never got rid of anything but trash.

"What do you call trash?" he asked. "Floor lamps?"

Yet to live where we were was enough to ask of existence. It was our first castle, this fishbowl, this exposed corner apartment where our bathroom was so near the front entrance that it caused a public uproar to flush the toilet. At night as B. and I slept, people moved to and fro on the sidewalk not three feet from our bed. I liked the sound of footsteps, preferring it to the swish of the sea. Passersby had many tempos. They bowled, strode, crept, clumped, tottered, staggered along, grunting to themselves in oxfords or arguing with their wives in high heels. If the footsteps stopped outside our Venetian blinds, I would wake with a start to hear a man whisper, "Aren't you going to kiss me good night?"

I stood at my front windows and saw the world—everyone I knew, like living in a small town. At noon the English Department poured out of Brown House and crossed the street, where the married men turned in at our building to lunch with their wives and the bachelors went on to the nearest lunchroom. They were my friends, waving to me as they passed. Last of all came B. arguing loudly with Harmon, disputing under the window for ten minutes till I knocked on the windowpane and called, "Go home, Harmon," and he threw me a kiss and ran down the street to his home on Sedgwick Avenue.

The doorman despised us from the start, a dour Scot named Andrew; but that was fair enough, tit for tat. The boys clattered in and out of the lobby. The toilet flushed in his ears. Twice when Moll and Sally spent an evening with us he threatened to call the police, notably one cater-wauling night when we tried to sing the Antonio Lotti eight-part "Crucifixus" with only four voices.

He must have been a Calvinist, the doorman, since only the elect got past his gates. A Jehovah's Witness, no matter how wiry and determined, stood no chance; he ousted many a prayermonger. Somehow only those meek inheritors of the earth, the sweetfaced nuns, slipped by him to solicit alms for the Church of St. Nicholas Tolentine.

I couldn't shut my door either on their saintly faces. They stood, two nuns together, peering inquisitively over my shoulder to see how neat my house was, asking gently impertinent questions like "Are you a recent bride, my dear?" ("No, Sister, I have two sons.") "Aren't you a little too young, child, to be married?" (I was thirty-five.)

Or the older one said shyly, "If you please, we would like to take a brief look round your apartment," the younger one nodded assent, and they tiptoed in and scurried from room to room, admiring everything, striking a tentative note on the piano, touching with wonder the pots and pans in the kitchen. Not till the end of the tour, as I gave them the money they had come for, did they inquire, "Are you one of Us?" then thanked me anyway and left with sweet forgiving smiles.

*

"If," said Mrs. Peterkin, "we could only be more wise as a family!" How could they manage it?
"It comes from books," said one of the family.

The children read everything from *The Peterkin Papers* to *Hamlet* (Pip slept on a copy of *Hamlet,* which he kept under his pillow), and I made myself hoarse reading to them. Also they were notetakers. When I arrived home in the late afternoon from the Browsing Room, David would meet me at the door and hand me a note:

How Bad Philip Was

1. He poot his feet on the piano keys
2. He got on top the piano
3. He was runing around so I codn't play the piano

Pip would address a chatty message to David sitting directly across the table from him:

Dear David
I do not think that bilding houses is worth it. Becase when you bild mother always comes and busts it down. If you think its wroth it answer.
Sincerely yours Philip

Next day Pip wrote to me:

Dear Helen
It is good that you have stopped busting down David's houses. If you hadn't it wold have been worse. But David seems to be busting them down. If David busts them down why does he worry? Love and Kisses from Philip R. Bevington

And David would dash off a message to cheer me on my trip to the grocery store: "I will try not to raise cane when you are away."

In the spring of 1940, B. again fell all but fatally ill with the old ailment, his third, most virulent attack of osteomyelitis—as it happened the last he ever had. After that prolonged siege, the killer let go, but not till it had made one more try to kill him.

When he returned from Orthopaedic Hospital, drained by suffering and immobilized by a plaster cast from ankle to hip, he had but a single desire in his head: to finish his doctoral thesis and be done. The bout with death had determined him. Even more, the worsening state of the world made every day a borrowed one. The hours of reckoning had come. It was no time to be fooling around with a study of a Victorian periodical and its effect on British opinion of a century ago.

As he lay in bed writing the final draft furiously in pencil, finishing a sheet and hurling it like a flaming taper across to the desk where I sat typing page after page for the printer—the world went thoroughly to pieces. The U-boats were sinking whole convoys of ships at sea. In April the Nazis punctually invaded Denmark and Norway, ticking off the countries. In May came the evacuation at Dunkirk, following the fall of Belgium and Holland. On June 14 the German armies marched into Paris, stricken France collapsed and fell ("And this is the way the world ends"). England would be next with none to rescue her; she stood at bay, alone. What could save that little island now? The Führer was spreading death over Europe in a new Occupation, preparing a new world order for a master race, a police state under the swastika of the Third Reich—a world of Hitler. And B.'s book was 415 pages long.

He wrote each night till the eleven o'clock news, then we listened to the radio and Edward R. Murrow saying, "This is London"—or, as holding my breath I waited to hear, "This is London *no more.*" Each night we learned the new words: Luftwaffe, Messerschmitt, Stuka, dive bomber, balloon barrage, flak, incendiaries, Spitfires, antiaircraft guns. And the old words: burning, burning, burning.

One had to stifle the imagination. It was something all soldiers must learn in order to survive, something Wilfred Owen in the First World War had called "insensibility," letting the veins run cold.

"Happy are these who lose imagination," he wrote, these who "Can laugh among the dying, unconcerned." Now civilians must learn it too, for the killing was impartial. Everyone had his own war to wage against the enemy.

Month by month the European war grew nearer, inescapable, while the isolationists hid like ostriches from it and the interventionists grimly sought it out. In November, 1940, came the crucial third-term struggle when Roosevelt won over Wendell Willkie. The Republicans called Roosevelt a dictator trying to destroy the capitalist system. He was the enemy of the people. He had betrayed his class and sold out the vested interests.

Before the election, our boys hastened home from the Barnard School wearing Republican buttons: "We Want Willkie." Once again B. might have said "I told you so," meaning what else can you expect of a private school?— especially when a neighbor, some partisan of Right and Justice, stopped him on the street to report the defection. "Mr. Bevington, do you know that your sons are wearing Willkie buttons?"

B. nodded. "I know," he said. "I let them do their own political thinking."

But he would have refused to live with me if I had failed to vote for Mr. Roosevelt. This time I did, a good Democrat at last, a good wife to B. He felt so keenly the need to a shaky planet of winning this election that even on our way to the polls he waylaid Harmon and pleaded with him to change his vote.

I laughed that morning to think how hard B. was working to save Harmon's soul, just as Harmon in the same spirit had tried, unsuccessfully, to save mine.

*

Like everyone else I ask myself: where was I when the tragedy happened? So one becomes part of a moment of history. When the news came in 1963 that John F. Kennedy was shot, I was weighing a pound of string beans at the A. & P. "They've killed the President," a man said behind me. "He's just been murdered in Texas." When Franklin D. Roosevelt died in 1945, I was rocking on a back porch in North Carolina. Both times I stopped to grieve and weep. When in 1941, on December 7 at Pearl Harbor, the war blazed up and exploded death in our faces, I know very well where I was. Whether it matters where I was depends, of course, on the point of view. In writing of oneself the answer is simple: it matters.

Professor Hunter Wright (as I began by saying on page one) taught a course in Romanticism at Columbia University. In 1927 he had innocently brought B. and me together in one classroom to hear him lecture on Jean Jacques Rousseau and under his nose carry on our love affair. In 1941 he took us hiking in the Catskill Mountains on the day of Pearl Harbor. Professor Wright also wrote a book on Wordsworth's "Ode on the Intimations of Immortality."

The day the war came, a Sunday, B. and I rose at 4:00 A.M. We slipped out of the apartment, leaving the two boys behind to do what they had agreed to do—eat their breakfast and go to stay with the McGees in the opposite wing who had offered to look after them.

We met Professor Wright before sunrise and drove with

him on a bitterly cold December morning (the kind he called tonic) ninety miles to the mountains, to a spot near Lake Mohonk high in the Catskills where we left the car parked in the snow to begin our daylong hike.

Professor Wright was a professional walker or zealot, a country man about as rugged as Thoreau but less solitary. His idea of a Sunday stroll was to gather some companions and take them in the dead of winter to the Catskills, there to wade to the hips in snow through mountain trails, climb rocks, follow ridges, and conquer a peak or two before sunset. He carried along two hardboiled eggs in a brown-paper bag for lunch and ate them on the move. On his advice we did the same. It was too cold anyway to stand still to eat a hardboiled egg. Though many admired him as a teacher and a Wordsworthian, few if any of his former students would walk with Professor Wright because of the enormous physical toll it took. B. and I went only once, and this was the time.

If we thought of it as a sentimental gesture, a literary pilgrimage with our dear old professor, we were quickly undeceived. This was no day for quoting English poetry or discussing the Romantic Movement. The appropriate debate was of chilblains, not belles lettres. Professor Wright kept up steam all day, flashing up and down the mountainside, plunging into snowdrifts, following a frozen stream, never lost but never really getting anywhere.

At six o'clock that evening, about dark, we finally wound up where we started, in front of his parked car—the most blessed sight I ever laid eyes on. Staggering like a dying person, by now numb with cold and congealed beyond the power of speech, I summoned up enough strength to crawl into the back seat and lie down. B. could still speak, though his voice sounded thin like a glacier and far off.

"By the way, Dr. Wright, how many miles do you figure we've gone in a complete circle?" he asked.

"Oh, not many, not many, something under thirty," said the Professor heartily. "The snow slowed us down, and I didn't want to overtax you. I believe in leisurely enjoyment of a walk, communing with Nature, so to speak. Like William and Dorothy. So, here we are."

He jumped nimbly into the car and put his foot on the starter. Nothing happened. Over the next half hour he went on trying, while B. tried profanity and prayer. It was altogether dark now. According to Professor Wright's pocket thermometer, it was five degrees above zero. The battery was dead. We would have to walk down off the mountain or die where we were.

I knew a song once: *"Tummel dich"*—move along.

The professor made this clear. "We'll have to keep moving," he said, "or freeze to death." By his flashlight he looked glassy-eyed. Even he was frightened and more than a little spent.

Move, *move,* keep on moving! I told myself as we started down in single file, not by the road but by his shortcut straight through the snow. He led the way, his light picking out the white trail below us. I walked in the middle, and my body was so stiff with cold that at each step I jerked along like a puppet, smothering a scream. With cramped leg muscles, it was an agony to move at all.

Five miles down the mountainside, this was the silent, dogged way we crept, just by taking the next step. Everything depended on taking the next step. It seemed a simple mortal thing, like facing the end of the world. Once more the familiar words, now strangely prophetic, rose up in my throat to choke me, and I whispered them to myself as I took the next step, and the next, and the next—

What if this present were the world's last night?
Marke in my heart, O Soule, where thou dost dwell

David and Philip would be home now from a double-feature movie, uneasy at our absence, then afraid, then terrified. But suppose it were the world's last night and we never returned at all. Suppose we never reached the end of the endless journey. Suppose—?

About nine o'clock that night we came down to a main highway and slowly followed it to a crossroads where, at a small filling station and general store, we were able to ask for help and whatever restoratives they kept in stock for survivors.

It was there we learned of the three thousand dead at Pearl Harbor.

*

I hadn't yet realized, at my age, that the end of the world comes regularly, many times in a lifespan. A world will end when it will—say, about every ten years? But I had learned something by that Sunday's experience: I knew now what single thing I wanted above all, with a compulsive desire. It was to get out of New York before it was too late. No matter now whether one believed in isolation or intervention, whether one believed in living or dying—the war had come. The shooting war.

It came next day after Pearl Harbor when we declared war on Japan; three days later Hitler and Mussolini declared war on us. Two decades after one world conflict we began again, and this time it was really global. The enemy was ours, the battlefield everywhere.

How long are one's memories—a day long? A life long? The mind snatches and lets go again. Yet the thoughts I kept of this black hour seem to return always in the same guise: stunned by fear. Was I such a coward then within myself, or was the threat real enough and sufficient? In those first stark months of 1942, everything spoke the danger (the Death March from Bataan in April, the fall of Corregidor in May, the struggle in June between Hitler and Stalin, now deadly enemies). Where were we? Reason told me to be afraid, a havoc in the head. Instinct said so, in the interstices of the mind.

"I will show you fear in a handful of dust."

"The tiger springs in the new year. Us he devours."

*

A few isolated scenes separate themselves out. One indelible memory is of an airraid drill at the Barnard School. We conducted these training exercises in lifesaving with dutiful regularity. Instead of telling the children to crawl under their desks when the bombs began to fall, we marched them out of the school building in an orderly file (like the oldfashioned fire drills of my childhood) and led them smartly to the opposite side of the street. There, with no shelter of any kind available, they stood ranged on the sidewalk under the sky—several hundred children in a long straggling line down the street. Without so much as an umbrella over their heads, they stood—the small targets—laughing and clowning around, mine with the rest, saved in their innocence from grasping the awful futility of the performance or how absurdly vulnerable they were.

On a midnight in the spring, the sirens gave the alarm for the other kind of airraid drill, one that affected the whole city. We had these drills regularly too, but this time the eerie sound was different. B. and I lay in our bed listening to the piercing wail of the sirens, aware of its meaning, of what dire warning it gave. "It's come at last," we whispered, the real event, a real airraid, with the German bombing planes already zooming in over Long Island. Then we turned on the radio to learn that a mistake in identification had been made, a false alarm. But that night settled it for me; I begged B. to carry us away from the threatened city, anywhere but here, preferably to another planet. He promised he would—to Venus, he said, not to Mars.

It look several months to bring the flight off. The June before, he had been granted his Ph.D. degree from Columbia, in a ceremony conducted by Nicholas Murray Butler to the sound of brass and the flourish of trumpets. Yet B. was no longer impressed by the academic procession. He wore the cap, the hood, the velvet-trimmed doctoral gown ruefully. His degree meant less to him than the fact that he was serving nightly on a draft board, Local No. 120 of the Bronx, as part of the war effort.

*

The chance to escape came that summer while we were in Vermont in a cottage at Sunset Lake. Ned Knowles, who was teaching in the summer school at New York University, lived in our Bronx apartment while we occupied his summer place. It was a lovely respite from the New York dimout, the screaming sirens, the tension, the jitters, the hoo-ha's. B. needn't spend his nights now remorseful at sending off young draftees to war. It was a lull from Lidice, wiped out by the Nazis on June 10, its men shot, all traces of a living town erased.

B. sat in a rocking chair on the porch overlooking the small lake, reading Homeric Greek. He had planned to learn Greek before he was ninety, and again the time seemed to grow dangerously short. I sat upstairs beside the window, trying to write verse, feeling more serene and happy than I had in years. Each of us kept an eye on the boys out in the rowboat fishing for perch. At intervals B. would leap from his chair, shout "Goddamn it, Dave, sit down in that boat!" sigh in content, and go back to rocking and reading the first book of the *Iliad*.

At Sunset Lake the offer came of an assistant professorship at Duke University in Durham, North Carolina. Once more the gods had heard and graciously intervened. They had granted a wish for rescue almost as soon as it was petitioned for.

We had a further prayer—that Durham, wherever it might be, would emerge a tiny village of not more than 800 inhabitants. The towns I had loved most as a child had been that size. Without ado we jumped into the car and drove the five miles to the nearest library at Orwell, Vermont. When B. opened the atlas, we studied the map to find out first where the state of North Carolina was. It turned out to be south of Virginia. Then he looked up the size of Durham.

"Oh, my God," B. groaned in disappointment, closing the book. "It's enormous. It has 60,195 inhabitants."

"It's bigger than New York," Pip said.

"We can't go," David said. He turned away sadly. "I wouldn't care for it at all."

*

We moved to North Carolina in August, 1942. We had lived in New York for sixteen years, B. and I, and now we were leaving it behind forever. It had to be forever. Yet all of my life that mattered to me, the part spent in loving B. and bearing his children, had happened in New York. My father Charley once advised me to be lucky, to have things my own way, and in this city I had obeyed him. Maybe the luck would hold in the South, a debatable land where none of us had set foot. You could never tell about luck (or was it cunning, only another word for survival?). It was hardly a thing to count on. Anyway, where B. went I was sure to go.

We had lived these years in parlous times, in turbulence—from the Roaring Twenties to the Depression Thirties to the Fighting Forties. From the crash of the Depression to the crash of Pearl Harbor. From the rise of Communism, Fascism, Nazism, from dictatorships and mass murders, to what would shortly become the Atomic Age. From World War II to what would become (would it, at last?) that final, total, cosmic nuclear war, World War III, and the end of the planet.

For our sons these were the times in which they were born, and in which they must try to survive in a new Age of Crisis. You would never call it a golden age. It was a bloody mess all around. With good reason it continued to grow and burgeon into another age of anxiety.

*

I am a rememberer, of course. And any rememberer is given to, and far better at, looking back rather than forward. Yet more than twenty years later—that is, only the other day—I asked a man the idle question one still continues to ask these uncertain days: what he would do if, hearing the last thundercrack, he knew it was already too late and we were about to reach an abrupt end on this planet. He answered with composure, and, as professors usually do, without a moment's hesitation.

"I would go out and dig in my garden," he said.

The answer, sensible and reassuring as it was, had a familiar ring. It was Martin Luther's choice, in a time of great stress: "If I knew that the world was coming to an end tomorrow, I would still plant my apple tree today."

It was Montaigne's whole philosophy. To live was for him *"mon métier, mon art."* Yet when in the sixteenth century the perils of his time confronted and threatened to engulf him, he said: "Let death come find me planting my cabbages, unconcerned by its coming and still less concerned for my unfinished garden."

"Cela est bien dit," repondit Candide, "mais il faut cultiver notre jardin."

That is well said, I thought, but some of us will undoubtedly face such a final moment of history totally unprepared, not a hoe within reach, not a garden rake to our name. In that case, I suppose the only other choice is to read a book.

The possibilities are large, too large to be speculated upon. Sydney Smith once said a man ought to live always in the best company when he reads. Preferably he ought to die so too. A few writers would be better avoided as unsavory company at world's end—Montesquieu, for example, with indifference in his heart, icicles in his ink, and the leisure of an empty hour of existence yet to spare. "I have never known a sorrow," wrote Montesquieu coldly, "that an hour's reading could not dissipate."

But there are others more congenial. Had I but world enough and time, I would choose to spend it with Thoreau or Mr. White of Selborne, neither of whom ever recorded a personal disaster or a sense of despair. Or with Jane Austen, who wrote six novels in which nobody died.

I might settle for a last lovely murmuration from Herrick:

Tumble me down, and I will sit
Upon my ruins (smiling yet)

Or depart boldly with the Wife of Bath:

Lat go, farewel! the devel go therwith.
The flour is goon, there is namore to telle.

Or reflect with Cummings:

the single secret will still be man . . .

what if a dawn of a doom of a dream
bites this universe in two,
peels forever out of his grave

182

and sprinkles nowhere with me and you? . . .
the most who die, the more we live

Or ask with Auden:

Do I love this world so well
That I have to know how it ends?

Grateful I would turn to Montaigne, who thought so highly of books as a source of solace and consolation. "They banish the clouds," he said. At least I would read on while the time allowed—nothing grandiose, nothing intemperate. Only a terrible swift word.

Perhaps it sounds like a foolish plan, even impractical. The idea of a book against the dark (and, finally, the closed book) is no doubt absurd; but then man is absurd also, as Camus revealed him—absurd man exalting life, seeking to behave rationally in an irrational world. Still, a word's eye view is not to my mind such a bad idea. To me there is in fact only the one view, whether of life or death. It is simple and eternally the same—a book and a love affair, that is all one needs. That is all one ever needs.

On the other hand, anyone who believes this, assenting to the supreme worth of these two, believes also in an undoomed planet and the permanence of love and the indestructibility of man. *Cras amet*. Tomorrow will be love.

"You see how it was," said B. "We had love. We loved each other."